Y0-DRV-486

"POWER TO COPE by Dr. Ross Rhoads is a practical and
helpful book by a dedicated pastor and experienced personal counselor. Based on his wide experience, this book
will be of assistance to all who have to cope with something. And that surely includes most of us."

Norman Vincent Peale
Foundation for Christian Living

* * *

"POWER TO COPE — it's the basic need in the lives of
Christians. Ross Rhoads is a gifted communicator who
does not waste his words or our time. I find this book
to the point, most practical, and compelling!"

Ben Haden, Speaker
Changed Lives TV-Radio
Chattanooga, Tennessee

POWER to COPE

ROSS RHOADS

Here's Life Publishers

Published by
Here's Life Publishers, Inc.
P.O. Box 1576
San Bernardino, CA 92402

HLP Product No. 951806
© 1987, Ross S. Rhoads
All rights reserved.
Printed in the United States of America.

Library of Congress Cataloging-in-Publication Data

Rhoads, Ross S. (Ross Stover), 1932-
    Power to cope.
      1. Christian life — 1960-   2. Life skills.
I. Hicks, Darryl E. II. Title.
BV4501.2.R485 1987   248.4   86-33480
ISBN O-89840-182-8

Unless otherwise indicated, Scripture quotations are from the *King James Version.*

Scripture quotations designated (NIV) are from *The Holy Bible, New International Version,* © 1978 by New York International Bible Society, published by the Zondervan Corporation, Grand Rapids, Michigan, and are used by permission.

Scripture quotations designated (AMP) are from *The Amplified Bible,* © 1965 by Zondervan Publishing House, Grand Rapids, Michigan, and are used by permission.

FOR MORE INFORMATION, WRITE:

L.I.F.E. — P.O. Box A 399, Sydney South 2000, Australia
Campus Crusade for Christ of Canada — Box 300, Vancouver, B.C., V6C 2X3, Canada
Campus Crusade for Christ — Pearl Assurance House, 4 Temple Row, Birmingham, B2 5HG, England
Campus Crusade for Christ — P.O. Box 240, Colombo Court Post Office, Singapore 9117
Lay Institute for Evangelism — P.O. Box 8786, Auckland 3, New Zealand
Great Commission Movement of Nigeria — P.O. Box 500, Jos, Plateau State Nigeria, West Africa
Campus Crusade for Christ International — Arrowhead Springs, San Bernardino, CA 92414, U.S.A.

SECOND PRINTING, APRIL 1988

To Carol, my wife,
who has given me peace in tribulation,
comfort in sorrow,
strength in weakness,
light in darkness,
and who has continued to love me
through all my dreams and doubts.

Acknowledgments

A special thanks must go to Marge Barton for her editing and proofreading prowess, and to the dedicated staff at Calvary Church for their encouragement, inspiration, and support.

Contents

POWER TO COPE

Ross Rhoads

1

POWER PARADOX

"I can't go on!" John's voice wavers as he speaks over the telephone. "Life is so unfair. I've given my life for others, and now that I'm facing problems, no one seems to care."

* * *

Mr. and Mrs. Smith are obviously troubled as they approach. "Where did we go wrong?" the pretty wife of the prestigious businessman begins, her eyes blinking back tears. "We've been faithful in church all these years. We've tried to do everything right for our children, to teach them — "

"And now," her husband blurts out, leaving much unexplained, "our lives are simply falling apart!"

"How could such a thing happen to *us?*" Mrs. Smith asks painfully.

* * *

From the beginning sentence, Martha's letter was

both terse and direct:

> It's all over! I just wanted you to be the first to know.
>
> I realize that by leaving Fred, everything that we've worked for will be destroyed, but I cannot take the situation any longer.
>
> I also understand that our Christian testimony will fall apart, too, but it has been a sham for many years anyway.
>
> I don't know what I will do with my life. All I know is that I cannot cope with the way things have been.
>
> Sincerely,
Martha

* * *

"John," "Mr. and Mrs. Smith," and "Martha," are all fictitious names. The stories, changed somewhat, are no-hope, real-life dramas. With different identities and settings, they are repeated every day throughout the modern world — from the largest cities to the most rural communities.

Like never before, we're surrounded by a society of answers and problem-solving gadgets, yet as individuals we seem less able than ever to cope with the challenges brought by today's changes.

"What's happening to me?" a typical American man asks confidentially. "Up until a year or so ago, I was a leader in my church and the community. I was happily married. I had few cares. But since that time, it seems as though the bottom has fallen out of my life. Everything that could possibly go wrong has. I feel like an empty shell."

UNABLE TO COPE

"I can't go on."
"Life is so unfair."
"Where did we go wrong?"
"How could such a thing happen to us?"
"I can't cope."
"What's happening to me?"
"I feel like an empty shell."

I *want* to give simple answers to horrendously hurting people, but, as a pastor and counselor, I *know* that people need more than churchy clichés and pious phrases. Not that there's a dearth of "help" for modern men and women. Consider the available newspaper articles, religious television and radio broadcasts, and the hundreds of new "overcoming life's problems" books that appear on our nation's bookshelves each year. We are barraged with potent "You can win" and "God wants the best for you" messages. Our pulpits and podiums resound with speakers who proclaim the win/win, power, and success doctrines.

By no means am I decrying this spreading phenomenon. Anyone who has heard me speak during the past twenty years knows how much I believe in the positive gospel. There can never be enough written or spoken on this great subject. But in the midst of the positive mental attitude teaching (religious and secular), I've noticed a nagging problem: We're faced with a paradox.

"PMA" speakers and preachers (and I count myself as one) have painted wonderful pictures of life's thrilling opportunities. Using vivid anecdotes and striking metaphors, we have sought to enlighten people in how to relish the colorful past, face the challenge of the present and dream of an exciting, goal-filled future. Christians have also been able to expound the added dimension of God's power and heaven's promises. With all these elements, how could we miss the secret of successful and fulfilled living?

Today's public, by and large, is a puzzled and disenchanted group. We are stronger because of the positive messages and books, but we wonder why we have so little power in our lives.

We're more aware of life's exciting opportunities, as evidenced in the parade of successful personalities we see on TV, hear on the radio and read about through the printed media. However, "John and Jane Christian" sit at home and wonder, *What's wrong with us? How come good things like that don't happen to us? Why doesn't everything always work out for the best in our lives?*

God cares for each person who has ever lived. Still, so many who believe in God feel relegated to some sort of "second-string" Christianity, trying hard but seeming to remain on the bottom rungs of life's ladder.

Indeed, we are faced with a paradox.

POWER

The Bible is permeated with references to extraordinary power. God, Himself, is power: "God hath spoken once; twice have I heard this, that power belongeth unto God" (Psalm 62:11).

God, according to His Word, has power to deliver, to fulfill promises, to subdue all things, to save to the uttermost, to keep us from falling, to use weak instruments and to deliver people from trouble. He also has the power to rule nature, to control the sea, to still tempests and stop the wind.

Christ, the embodiment of God the Father, revealed

His potency to save, to pardon, to give life, to work wonders and to lay down His life as a sacrifice for the sins of mankind. "And Jesus came and spake unto them, saying, 'All power is given unto me in heaven and in earth'" (Matthew 28:18). The Bible, God's Word, has that kind of power:

> For the Word that God speaks is alive and full of power — making it alive, operative, energizing and effective; it is sharper than any two-edged sword, penetrating to the dividing line of the breath of life (soul) and [the immortal] spirit, and of joints and marrow [that is, of the deepest parts of our nature] exposing and sifting and analyzing and judging the very thoughts and purposes of the heart (Hebrews 4:12, AMP).

More amazingly, as Jesus instructed, believers have this power available: "But you shall receive power — ability, efficiency and might — when the Holy Spirit has come upon you; and you shall be My witnesses in Jerusalem and all Judea and Samaria and to the ends — the very bounds — of the earth" (Acts 1:8, AMP).

Furthermore, Jesus made it clear that we would have supernatural power: "I tell you the truth, anyone who has faith in me will do what I have been doing. He will do even greater things than these, because I am going to the Father" (John 14:12, NIV).

With all that power, how could we miss? What could go wrong? Still we cry, often in desperation, "What's wrong with me?" Faced with life's problems, we apply all the self-help and spiritual principles we know; yet we seem powerless. What's the problem?

There are many different kinds of power. A wealthy person, for example, has intrinsic power because of his monetary clout. The President of the United States has designated power, an authority backed up inherently by his office. (This is similar, in a spiritual sense, to the inherited power of a believer: "But as many as received him, to them gave he power to become the sons of God, even to them that believe on his name" [John 1:12].)

In today's world, we see many forms of abused power — leaders of terrorist countries, Satan and his evil forces, and even well-meaning people who seek to manipulate others for a self-justified end.

Christians are sometimes guilty of a false assumption of power, claiming an undue authority over Satan (comparing the evil one to a toothless, haggard lion with nothing left but his roar). Certainly we do have rights, and God has clearly instructed us in how to deal with evil, but our power is limited: "Be well-balanced — temperate, sober-minded; be vigilant *and* cautious at all times, for that enemy of yours, the devil, roams around like a lion roaring [in fierce hunger], seeking someone to seize upon and devour" (1 Peter 5:8, AMP).

Satan still has much power. He hasn't yet been imprisoned. He continues to wreak havoc throughout the world.

> Withstand him; be firm in faith [against his onset] — rooted, established, strong, immovable and determined — knowing that the same (identical) sufferings are appointed to your brotherhood (the whole body of Christians) throughout the world (1 Peter 5:9, AMP).

WINNING

Christians sometimes think of power as a dominant, overwhelming force. Therein is the paradox, for not everybody in Christendom has been "winning" from the world's perspective. Stephen, the first Christian martyr, for example, died as stones pounded his body. However, his face was shining like an angel's. His innermost strands were strong. He was awesome in power, but the Christians of his day observed only a senseless death.

Stephen had been the primary lay person, as recorded in Acts 6-7, to stand before the Jerusalem council and preach what was probably the greatest sermon in the New Testament (an entire chapter — receiving more copy than the virgin birth of Jesus Christ).

It makes no sense, therefore, for Stephen to have died that way. Certainly there was no "winning" in being stoned to death. No blessing came from it that we can see. Saul (later called Paul) was there, probably calling the shots, but he continued to purge more Christians. The persecutor was saved eventually, but there's little evidence that his conversion was due to Stephen's martyrdom.

Stephen had power, but he was murdered because of his faith. All the positive thinking and affirmative confession cannot make an apparently senseless death like that disappear from the Bible's pages.

Paul, one of the most potent preachers and writers in history, was full of power. Yet he was beheaded in Rome. Much of the current teaching about "winning" and "faith" is taken from the apostle Paul's letters, but the writer died in apparent failure. In his final letter written from a stark prison cell in Rome, Paul told Timothy of his loneliness and the desertion of inconsistent associates. Paul asked his young friend to "bring his cloak and to come before winter," but the great apostle was brought before Nero and killed before he saw Timothy again.

The anguishing picture of a heavy Roman ax severing

Paul's head from his body is hardly a victorious sight. Witnesses to the grisly scene would never call Paul a "winner."

Today, as during the past two thousand years, Christians are faced with this troubling paradox. They are supposed to have the power to "win," but not every Christian appears to be winning. People are hearing positive, faith-filled messages and are learning to say all the right phrases, yet the mountains not only refuse to budge, but worse still, the barriers continue to grow and loom overhead.

Christian shepherds often talk about power and faith. Such subjects are pulpit favorites. Phrases such as "Keep on keeping on" (implying, "Don't act like it hurts") and "Keep a stiff upper lip" flow dramatically even though the flocks keep smacking repeatedly into the same problems.

MAINTAINING

There's another power about which we seldom teach — the power of maintaining, of enduring. Briefly put, there is *power in suffering*. Every great faith teacher quoted in the Bible experienced incredible struggles. That sort of "hang tough" power seems woefully out of date today.

Ninety-five percent of the book of Job encourages God's followers to have faith when all hope seems gone. Throughout the Scriptures, likewise, we find little that fits into today's positive thinking categories.

In fact, many times we're told (in today's terms) to quit crying, to get on with life. Everything isn't always going to be positive and victorious.

But does that mean we don't have the power God

promised? Were Paul and Stephen spiritual cripples because they met failure (or what seemed to be failure)? It's a paradox.

FACING PROBLEMS

When faced with problems, do we love and trust God, or are our words of faith merely empty, pious phrases? Faith, like power and suffering, is just a word until it's pressed into action. True faith must be applied continuously, even when trouble "rains and pours" on our lives.

The worst trials usually come at the most inopportune times. What if there are no easy-to-accept solutions for us? Too often the evangelically affluent try to have all the answers — to make all the jagged puzzle pieces fit together, leaving no place in our theology for the ugly or blemished.

Still, God has a place and purpose for everything. So what do we do when faced with serious personal problems, whether they be physical, moral, spiritual, mental, familial, social, or business-related? When our problems are so great that we feel as if the walls are caving in on us and that no one, not even God, seems to hear our cries for help, what do we do?

"And we know that all things work together for good to them that love God, to them who are the called according to his purpose" (Romans 8:28). What exactly was God teaching as He spoke those words through Paul's pen? Power to suffer? Power to tough it out? What kind of power are Christians supposed to exhibit?

For even to this were you called — it is inseparable
from your vocation. For Christ also suffered for

you, leaving you (His personal) example, so that
you should follow on in His footsteps (1 Peter 2:21,
AMP).

And the God of all grace, who called you to his
eternal glory in Christ, after you have suffered a
little while, will himself restore you and make you
strong, firm and steadfast. To him be the power
for ever and ever. Amen (1 Peter 5:10,11, NIV).

*Obviously, God is more interested in the growth of
His children than in their comfort.* He knows that our
faith develops when it's tested, and we find that He is
true to His word and all-sufficient. This process can be
painful, but it's far better than staying comfortable and
never maturing. Just as a child must grow, often through
struggle and difficult experience, so must we in our
spiritual lives.

PARADOX

The word *paradox* has appeared many times in the
preceding pages. It is, according to Webster, "a statement
that seems contradictory or absurd, but may be true in
fact." Does "toughing it out" as a Christian mean that
one cannot be a happy, positive-thinking overcomer?

We can overcome, but not always in the win/win
sense. To do so, we must face our problems with a
realistic examination of the tough times. Despite strained
relationships, we may be called upon to forgive and
release the hurt, though doing so doesn't necessarily
mean we'll immediately feel good about it. Job's kind of
trust causes us to believe in postponed resolutions and
delayed gratification. As we eventually pull away from
our protective shells, we can learn to give, not merely
take. As we take affirmative action, we can draw upon

the tremendous resources in God's Word.

Frankly, that can be difficult — but faith is more than a placebo. Even so, wounds leave scars, the hurts don't always go away and Christianity isn't fun all the time.

What happens, then, when we're faced with serious, horrible problems? Can we transpose God's promises into our own struggles? Can we truly face life without faking it?

> For God did not give us a spirit of timidity — of cowardice, of craven and cringing and fawning fear — but (He has given us a spirit) of power and of love and of calm and well-balanced mind and discipline and self-control. Do not blush or be ashamed then to testify to and for our Lord, nor of me, a prisoner for His sake, but (with me) take your share of the suffering (to which the preaching) of the Gospel (may expose you, and do it) in the power of God (2 Timothy 1:7,8, AMP).

Power, like faith, is more than a word, and it must be lived. Power is alive and energizing! Actions, not pious phrases, validate a person's trust in God.

It's a puzzling paradox: As believers in the Lord, we are both powerful and powerless. No one except God knows how all the pieces fit together. There are no easy answers, of course, but there is power to cope, as we'll see in the following chapter.

POWER PRINCIPLES

I can face life and its challenges through trusting in God's grace, even during the times when I feel most powerless.

I can best release my apprehensions about life's struggles by being forgiving, even to those who have hurt me.

I can rely on God's instruction, always realizing He is more interested in my growth than in my comfort.

I can strengthen my grip on life by reaching out to others, even in the midst of my own problems.

A POWER PROMISE

And after you have suffered a little while, the God of all grace — Who imparts all blessing and favor — Who has called you to His [own] eternal glory in Christ *Jesus*, will Himself complete *and* make you what you ought to be, establish *and* ground you securely, *and* strengthen (and settle) you (1 Peter 5:10, AMP).

A PRAYER FOR POWER TO COPE WITH TODAY (AND TOMORROW)

Lord, thank You for loving me, even when I was unlovable. Thank You for pardoning me, though I didn't deserve Your grace.

Now, Father, help me to trust You today and tomorrow. Even though I have little control over what will happen, I can rely on You. You alone are totally reliable.

Give me power to cope today — that enduring power — I pray. Amen.

2

POWER TO COPE
WITH FEAR

"**F**ear," Wordsworth wrote, "has a hundred eyes and they all agree to plague your heart."

Fear is a problem common to everyone. A painful, tragic emotion that's seldom helpful, it plagues our lives, fills entire hospital communities with severely disturbed patients, and robs otherwise happy people of their confidence and normal relationships. Fear breeds in almost every situation, growing in the roots of our lives and surviving on the doubts in our hearts.

PHOBIAS

According to a recent report in *USA Today*, more than five million Americans suffer from distinguishable phobias, including these most common fears:

Achlophobia (crowds)
Acrophobia (heights)
Aeremophobia (being alone)
Aerophobia (flying on planes)
Agoraphobia (open spaces, the marketplace)
Algophobia (pain)

Anthrophobia (people)
Claustrophobia (enclosed spaces)
Dentalphobia (dentists)
Ecclesiaphobia (churches)
Entomophobia (insects)
Gephyrophobia (bridges)
Graphophobia (writing in public)
Hematophobia (blood)
Hydrophobia (water)
Mysophobia (contamination)
Nosophobia (disease)
Nyctophobia (darkness)
Ophidiophobia (snakes)
Photophobia (light)
Scopophobia (being stared at)
Thalassophobia (ocean)
Topophobia (performing or public speaking)
Toxophobia (poisoning)
Trypanophobia (needles)
Zoophobia (animals)

So many of us are beset by these irrational, excessive, persistent fears. We're afraid of standing in line in stores, or of driving on highways — particularly potentially crowded freeways. We fear being away from the safety of home. Others of us cannot shower by ourselves because of fear. Elevators or public restrooms set some of us in a dither. Many of us who come to church must sit in the back near the aisles so we can retreat quickly if necessary.

Phobia victims share similar symptoms. For most, the chest and stomach tighten (some call this "getting butterflies"). Others have accompanying sweatiness, particularly on the palms. One's heartbeat quickens. The knees and legs weaken ("rubberlegs"). The mouth gets dry, and anguished breathing adds to the tension as hyperventilation is feared.

Beyond that, as millions well know, dizziness and shakiness occur. The vision becomes distorted as disorientation develops, and sometimes overwhelming panic encases the victim.

Dr. Arthur B. Hardy, president of the Phobia Society of America, describes anxiety this way:

> A phobia becomes so severe that the physiological reaction of the body incapacitates the person so that he can't run or defend himself. All people can do is try to get themselves away from the area (or cause) as fast as possible so they can get some relief from the horrible sensation that these physiological changes in the body are causing.[1]

Fears can be caused by uncertainty, ignorance, conflict or past experiences that traumatized the individual. However, many feel that fear is a learned behavior and that well-meaning parents often teach children to be afraid by making thoughtless, negative remarks (e.g., "Don't go near the water or you'll drown!").

Naming or identifying a fear doesn't automatically offset it, either. Knowledge generally brings freedom, but that isn't necessarily the case with fear, for it has an awesome power. When it strikes (such as a strange sound in the night), a person is usually incapable of responding to reason until some time has passed uneventfully.

Fear is a form of obsession, often irresistible and uncontrollable. It rises up in the strangest ways, responding to a wide variety of stimuli (i.e., when a person walks down a hospital corridor to visit a friend and gets that queasy, uncomfortable fear of "catching" something and becoming ill). One sometimes experiences fear before recognizing what it is. Fear comes cloaked illusively in so many forms — violence, aggression, impatience, hysteria, and anger, to name just a few.

How, then, can we face our fears?

NO EASY ANSWERS

The Bible contains more than 1500 references to fear, including Psalm 27:1: "The LORD is my light and my salvation; whom shall I fear?"

Whom (and what) shall we fear?

"Many things!" we answer. Today, it seems, we're surrounded by deep, shadowy valleys and have trouble puppeting the psalmist when he said, "I will fear no evil: for thou art with me" (Psalm 23:4).

In order to adequately face life and deal with our hounding fears, we need a friend, a redeemer. Jesus Christ is that friend and redeemer, the victor over our fears! It is Jesus who looks inside our hearts and sees our needs. Matthew's writings present a clear assurance of the Savior:

> Fear not them which kill the body, but are not able to kill the soul: but rather fear him which is able to destroy both soul and body in hell . . . Whosoever therefore shall confess me before men, him will I confess also before my Father which is in heaven . . . He that loveth father or mother more than me is not worthy of me: and he that loveth son or daughter more than me is not worthy of me. And he that taketh not his cross, and followeth after me, is not worthy of me. He that findeth his life shall lose it: and he that loseth his life for my sake shall find it (Matthew 10:28,32,37-39).

Jesus Christ saw people (then and now) as "sheep without shepherds," approaching precipices from which there could be no return. It is important to note that He referred to people as sheep, an animal legally blind, totally defenseless, easily led, unattractive, smelly — hardly the pretty picture we would paint of ourselves.

We seem leaderless. Without God, we cannot find the best way. As we become more aware of ourselves, more knowledgeable of our psychological tendencies, our fears are heightened. We realize, if we're truthful, our own incapacities and limitations.

In recent years, for example, we have seen the escalation of technology related to space exploration. Although outer space is only sixty miles away, closer than the distance from Charlotte to Winston-Salem, North Carolina, we fear it because it seems so foreign. The more we realize our finiteness, the more exaggerated are our fears of what's "out there." Without a trust factor and a source of help, our fears are intensified.

PROPER FEAR

"Fear not them which kill the body, but are not able to kill the soul: but rather fear him which is able to destroy both soul and body in hell" (Matthew 10:28). Fear, in this context, means "a reverential trust" or "an awesome appreciation for God." Reportedly, the ancient copiers of the sacred Scriptures possessed such a great awe of God that when they approached the word *Jehovah*, they would take up a quill that had never before been used.

Perhaps that seems extreme, but maybe we've lost much of our God-centered foundation because of our flippancy. "Stand in awe, and sin not," wrote the psalmist (Psalm 4:4). "Let all the earth fear the LORD: let all the inhabitants of the world stand in awe of him" (Psalm 33:8).

"Let us hear the conclusion of the whole matter," wrote wise Solomon. "Fear God, and keep his commandments: for this is the whole duty of man" (Ecclesiastes 12:13). Again quoting King David, "The fear of the LORD is the beginning of wisdom" (Psalm 111:10). Although it seems like a contradiction in terms, the best antidote for human fear (and bondage to it) is a reverent fear (awe) of God. If we're to be wise and balanced, we must have a healthy respect and a veneration for God, recognizing His whole awesomeness and sovereignty. He is the Almighty One!

"Fear not!" God commands, yet He also exhorts, "Fear Me."

That word *fear* appears in the Bible the first time in the book of Genesis, the last time in Revelation.

"Do not be afraid," Jesus says. "But to overcome fear, you must fear Me! Reverence Me! I am God! I am able to deliver you."

CONFESSION

"Whosoever therefore shall confess me before men, him will I confess also before my Father which is in heaven" (Matthew 10:32). Why would confession of Christ fit into the same portion of Matthew's letter where the disciple wrote "Fear not"? The reason is simple: God never provides a negative without offering a positive. Nothing but negatives would form a crippling psychological and spiritual vacuum.

Confession creates action, which inspires confidence and courage. Ridding ourselves of fear sometimes takes more than just a decision not to be afraid.

Salvation, for example, involves more than a desire

(and decision) to avoid a Saviorless life. On the positive side, confession of Christ confronts fear and creates hope and courage, especially when shared with others.

Beyond that, healing of fear through salvation requires that we share the joy of our redemption, not merely keeping it to ourselves (that is, confessing it). If we can help reproduce a Christ-experience in others, and if we align ourselves with Him through our confession, we then stand in the presence of the great confidence builder whose name is Jesus:

> A name which is above every name: that at the name of Jesus every knee should bow, of things in heaven, and things in earth, and things under the earth; and every tongue should confess that Jesus Christ is Lord, to the glory of God the Father (Philippians 2:9-11).

LOVE

Referring again to that passage in Matthew, Jesus coupled "Fear not" and "Confess Me" with another element — "Love Me." He used a shocking contrast, saying (in effect), "Compared to Me, everything else must diminish. Give me your fervor, your passion, your commitment, your loyalty, your sacrifice and your life."

In fact, according to Jesus, the true, permanent cure for fear is love, God's love. "God is love. Whoever lives in love lives in God, and God in him . . . There is no fear in love. But perfect love drives out fear" (1 John 4:16,18, NIV). Many phobias are related to an obsession with self. ("I am afraid of losing my husband." "I cannot drive my car for fear of wrecking it.") When we forget self and reach out in love, that love replaces the stagnancy with life-giving nourishment.

31

The smallest of victories over fear can give hope to the multitudes of people living with phobias. When we hand our obsession with self over to God, victories begin for us.

FOLLOW

In the previously mentioned section of Matthew, the "Fear not," "Confess Me" and "Love Me" phrases were topped with one final exhortation — "Follow Me." What a tremendous emphasis He places on a commitment to long-term action!

Man is prone, by nature, to his visible world. His tendency is to either ignore or fear the unseen. That very nature is a serious problem. Man seems to abhor commitment to an invisible God. This is where the element of faith must enter. The person who desires to overcome his fears must believe that Jesus "is a rewarder of them who diligently seek Him" (see Hebrews 11:6).

Having power over fear is not an end in itself. It is merely part of the progression toward total discipleship, for as Jesus said, "If you don't follow Me, you aren't being My disciple."

Quoting Arthur Hardy (the Phobia Society president) once more:

> There is no reason nowadays . . . that anybody has to suffer for a period of years. Now the ones who don't recover seem to be the ones who are passive. If you are passive, you don't get over much of anything. You don't get yourself a job (for example) if you just sit on your rear end and don't do anything. You're able to get over it if you face it and fight it.[2]

On a spiritual plane, there's an abandonment of self

that comes from a commitment to action (taking up my cross and following Him). That abandonment provides a vital, unknown quality in helping us overcome fears. We don't really know why it works. All we know is that it is effective.

The most famous passion play in the world is given by the people of the village of Oberammergau, Bavaria, in southern West Germany. It's performed as a result of a vow made by the villagers in 1633. At the time, a plague raged in the neighborhood, and when it ended, the people of the area gratefully promised to honor the Passion of Christ by giving a play. They have kept that vow and performed the play every ten years since. The play lasts eight hours and includes more than 1200 performers.

Of late, Antone is the man who has been chosen to portray Christ. Those who have seen the presentation agree that his depiction literally transfixes the audience. "It is almost," one person related, "as if I were actually there at Golgotha some two thousand years ago!"

An American tourist (leave it to an American) reportedly went backstage one time while Antone was removing his costume. Gesturing toward the cross Antone had carried, the intruder asked, "May I touch and lift it?"

The actor nodded, then watched as the tourist put his shoulder under the cross and strained to lift the timbers. "Wow!" the American exclaimed. "That cross is really heavy. It must be made of solid oak."

"Of course," Antone said. "Unless I can feel the weight of the cross on my back, I cannot play Christ's part correctly."

The Lord Jesus Christ, in encouraging us to unmask and release our fears, offers us more than a stale vacuum.

We are to confess Him. We must love Him and follow Him. He doesn't dole out polished, glistening, stylish crosses. He points us away from the styrofoam, easily-destructed crosses and gives us the rugged, solid beams of burden.

Why does God use such a troublesome process to help us overcome fear? Simply put, struggle gives us power — an inner strength — to face other quests. "Behold, God is my salvation; I will trust, and not be afraid: for the LORD JEHOVAH is my strength and my song; he also is become my salvation" (Isaiah 12:2).

POWER PRINCIPLES

I can face my fears through a realistic examination of the causes.

I can release those fears through forgiveness of those who may have initiated my apprehension.

I must trust God to help me cope with my fears, still realizing He is more interested in my growth than in my comfort.

I can strengthen my healing from fear by reaching out to others — even in the midst of my own hurts.

A POWER PROMISE

The LORD is on my side; I will not fear: what can man do unto me? (Psalm 118:6)

A PRAYER FOR POWER TO COPE WITH FEAR

Father, I give You thanks that You sent Your Son, the Lord Jesus, whose name is above every other name.

I confess my fear, specifically _____ , and I proclaim that You are able to help me cope with and overcome that fear.

Help me to trust You. Help me not to worry about things over which I have little or no control. Help me to realize that You are working everything out for my good, even when I don't understand.

Give me power to cope with fear — Your inner, enduring power — I pray, with thanksgiving. Amen.

3

POWER TO COPE
WITH FAILURE

Too often we look at other people's lives through rose-colored glasses. We talk about Sylvester Stallone's "overnight success" with the first "Rocky" movie, for example, and we forget that he struggled against the motion picture establishment for years trying to get someone excited about the project.

We listen to the latest album by country singer Lee Greenwood and flippantly remark, "I never heard of him a few years ago; where did he come from? I wonder how he became a star so quickly?" But we may not realize that Lee "paid his dues" for more than a decade in relative obscurity.

We thrill to see Fernando Valenzuela hurl his famous screwball for the Los Angeles Dodgers, but we seldom hear about the years he spent as a teenager traveling with an itinerant baseball team over dusty Mexican back roads.

The American public has made Lee Iaccoca's life story a best-selling book. He basks in the glory of public adulation. However, only a few years ago, he was disdained by the media and portrayed as a villain in the loan-guarantee controversy surrounding the almost-certain bankruptcy of the Chrysler Corporation.

"Success" stories have been that way throughout history. Vincent Van Gogh sold only one painting in his entire lifetime, and that was to his own brother. The classic portrait "Whistler's Mother," when submitted to the Royal Academy, was quietly relegated to the gallery's cellar and remained there for many years.

Rudyard Kipling, since heralded as one of the world's greatest poets, was passed over three times for poet laureate of Great Britain because an obscure line in one of his verses had offended Queen Victoria.

The operas "Madame Butterfly," "Fidelia," and "Rite of Spring" were all miserable flops on their respective opening nights, but have since become operatic classics, gracing most of the world's great stages.

Now considered the world's most popular board game, "Monopoly" was flatly rejected by the leading game company. Authorities claimed that it contained dozens of "serious faults" that would prevent it from becoming a success. That was millions of copies ago.

James Joyce's collection of short stories, *Dubliners*, was turned down by at least twenty-two publishers before it was finally accepted by a relatively unknown company.

The Decca Recording Company turned down the Beatles in 1962, even after the group had experienced incredible audience response in England and Europe. An official with the company made the now-laughable statement, "We don't like their sound. Besides, groups of guitarists are on the way out!"

SCARS

Unfortunately, all stories don't contain success-filled anecdotes. Throughout history, the biographies of both well-known and obscure people contain many scars. Truthfully, failure is as much a part of life as success. Someone once said, "Anyone who boasts that he has no regrets is depending on two bad memories — his and ours!" Some people rebound from discouragement and defeat, but many cannot overcome the vicious failure cycle.

The fear of failure is in itself debilitating. That man or woman who expects to fail most likely will. When a person continues to experience failure, he develops a trend — another link in the chain. Soon he's relying on a negative reservoir, with any action or willingness to try again coming from a position of weakness more than strength.

We are the extended shadows of our backgrounds, our experiences, our fears, our hopes. All these elements play roles in what we are and do today.

What makes the difference, then, between life's winners and losers? How can one become a success despite repeated failures?

FACING THE FACTS

Failure is all around us. Listening to and reading the news, one is quickly reminded of society's breakdowns and the "bad luck" that has befallen people — the accidents, tragedies, deaths, bank robberies, unemployment statistics, and bloodshed. Why, then, do some people succumb to such disparaging events while others see the proverbial roses among the thorns?

One of the greatest differences I've seen between

winners and whiners is this: *accountability.* Excuses have no lasting value; the person who fails often relies on such a Band-Aid mentality (and there are lots of "reasons" for failures). But the overcomer admits his defeat, learns from his mistakes and heads in the right direction. Henry Ford, the automobile magnate, once said, "Failure is only the opportunity to begin again, more intelligently."

The temptation to look for a scapegoat rather than a solution is entirely normal. But a true success looks inside a situation for answers. He finds that behind every defeat is hope, and that failure can sometimes be the best teacher. He admits that failure is often "normal," the common bond of human nature.

An overcomer will soon realize the importance of observing other people, knowing he can learn from them, but also knowing that when the tough decisions have to be made, he must be accountable for his own actions. A failure, on the other hand, may find his own shortcomings or personal flaws difficult to deal with or admit, preferring to lay the blame on other people or things.

Defeat must be faced. Our greatest glory consists not in never failing, but in admitting our mistakes while determining to continue in spite of our past shortcomings.

REALISM

One of the common fallacies concerning failure, especially among Christians, comes into play when a person disregards a realistic approach to overcoming his failures, expecting instant perfection. For example, a man may have had a problem with alcoholism for years. When he admits his failure and asks God for help, he may not experience instant restoration for his loss of control and its effects. He could become very discouraged if he doesn't face the problem realistically.

A couple may have been destroying the marital bond (in any number of ways) for years, yet when they finally seek God's help in "patching things up," they cannot understand why the marital bliss doesn't return instantly. God doesn't always give immediate healing, nor does He conveniently "patch things up" on demand. Some situations may never be as they were before.

We live in a quick-fix society. The grocery store is filled with "instants": potatoes, rice, pastries, microwave popcorn, TV dinners, and ready-to-serve desserts. We live in modular homes and drive automobiles with electronic ignitions, automatic transmissions, power steering and push-button, multiplex radios. We drive these "instant" cars through two-minute car washes, then rush over to eat at one of the many fast food restaurants so we can hurry home to switch on the remote control, instant-picture television program being beamed in a microsecond from a station to our home.

But God doesn't cater to our instant-cure mentalities. His ways are not our ways, and His timing is not measured by human clocks. A person may say, "God, I admit my sin. I was wrong. I'm not going to do that anymore." Still, the healing may be a drawn-out process. As God helps him grow, that person will probably go through a period of struggles whether he has failed in a business venture, marriage, or some other personal relationship.

A parent who becomes a Christian may go to his grown children and profess his new faith in Christ. But if for twenty years he's been a terror in the home, his children may not immediately accept his story or his Savior. That's a tough truth. Our God, the Great Physician, has the power to perform quick fixes today, but seldom, even when the Bible was being written, did He choose instant methods for helping men and women overcome failure. God *does* forgive and forget. Our failures don't have to remain stumbling stones. But no one can revoke the past, and only God can turn defeats into stepping stones.

Helen Keller, one of the twentieth century's foremost overcomers, wrote the following revelation:

> There may have been errors that cannot be corrected; injuries that cannot be repaired; losses that cannot be redeemed; stains that cannot be removed; words that cannot be recalled; but which are like birds set loose in the forest.
>
> Remorse cannot empty our jails, or bring back the dead, or unwrite what has been written.[1]

Still, hope reigns supreme, even among life's worst defeats. "For thou, LORD, are good, and ready to forgive; and plenteous in mercy unto all them that call upon thee" (Psalm 86:5).

STARTING OVER

Behind every defeat is the promise of new opportunity. George Frederick Handel learned that. For forty years he had been the most sought-after composer of operatic music among England and Europe's elite. Fame so frequently is fickle, however, and Handel fell upon hard times. In 1741, on a hot day in August, aged and penniless, he wandered through the streets of London, dejected and defeated.

Then Handel was stricken with a cerebral hemorrhage that paralyzed one side of his body. He couldn't walk. The physicians gave little hope. The musician's malady brought more self-pity and bitterness.

One day Charles Gibbon, a wealthy poet, visited the despondent Handel. He gave George a manuscript with the text taken from the Bible. Gibbon suggested that his composer friend work with it.

At first Handel looked over the text with scorn, but his face changed visibly as he leafed through the pages. He was especially moved by a portion of Scripture from Isaiah: "He is despised and rejected of men. He looked for someone to have pity on Him, but there was no one; neither found He any to comfort Him."

The words consumed the musician's personal hurt. On and on he read until reaching the lines, "I know that my Redeemer liveth. Rejoice. Hallelujah!"

Handel reached for a pen. For twenty-one days, with few interruptions, he wrote "The Messiah." Tears repeatedly blinded his vision as he wrote. "I did think I did see all heaven before me," he blurted, "and the Great God Himself."

The new composition was first presented in London. King George II was in attendance. During the final part of the performance, the monarch was so gripped with emotion that he rose to his feet. Naturally his subjects stood with him, and thus began the tradition whereby audiences rise during the "Hallelujah Chorus."

It was a triumph born out of defeat. Handel enjoyed his renewed success, though age continued to grip him. He went blind, but for the final six years of his life, the great composer's faith never again wavered. "The Messiah" and its victorious theme had become personal reality in George Frederick Handel's life.

FAILURE IS NOT LOSS

Though all of us cannot pen a heralded composition, we can find the flicker of hope among life's smoldering ashes if we desire to do so. It's at night that astronomers discover new heavenly bodies. Similarly, it's often during the blackness and bleakness of defeat that people discover new glimmers of hope.

To the objective critic, humanly speaking, Jesus failed. After the ultimate rejection, He was pitifully crucified. But that "failure" fulfilled hundreds of prophecies, and His sacrificial death brought the gift of eternal life to anyone who would believe in His saving love.

> In whom we have redemption through his blood, the forgiveness of sins, according to the riches of his grace (Ephesians 1:7).
> But God commendeth his love toward us, in that, while we were yet sinners, Christ died for us (Romans 5:8).
> Be imitators of God, therefore, as dearly loved children and live a life of love, just as Christ loved us and gave himself up for us as a fragrant offering and sacrifice to God (Ephesians 5:1,2, NIV).

Starting over again, though sometimes supremely difficult, can be the greatest experience in the world, though it may be a while before a person realizes the importance of overcoming failure.

The possibilities of a fresh, new beginning can spark excitement, regardless of the problems leading to the defeat. Failure can diminish quickly as a person builds a new foundation for success.

QUITTING

There is much truth to the phrase that finds its way into nearly every coach's pep-talk: "A quitter never wins, and a winner never quits." In all accuracy, however, a quitter does win sometimes, and a winner may quit at times. The difference lies in the overall strategy.

One of the greatest reasons people don't overcome defeat is rather simple — they give up. Many, in fact, are not so much failures in life as they are people who never succeed. In our transient society, the temptation arises often to go from job to job, relationship to relationship, and place to place, constantly giving in to the usually false presumption that the grass is always greener on the other side of the fence. Change for change's sake is not always better. The results of jumping from one situation to another are often feelings of frustration and lack of self-confidence.

There's a God-created need within each of us that thrives on achieving success through completing the tasks we begin. Quitting interrupts the process toward fulfillment. Each new effort or venture becomes weakened subconsciously by the past experience of failing to finish. This flaw increasingly spoils the prospect of completion.

The same applies to the spiritual realm. People may readily desire to accept God's plan for their lives. They begin reading the Bible, offering prayers, seeking Christian fellowship and looking for new direction for the future. However, some believers, because they cannot (or will not) make lasting commitments, are doomed to fail almost from the beginning.

FOUNDATIONS

We need stability. The degree to which mankind

lives without absolutes and ultimate meaning is the degree to which man will sense his lostness and instability.

Overcoming defeat is something like constructing a building. No matter what existed on that property before, a great structure can be built if the foundation is strong enough. (Disney World, for instance, was built on what was previously a boggy Florida swamp.) Mankind needs a foundation that overcomes the ashes of failure. The wise person establishes solid building blocks in his life as he seeks to live successfully.

There are many references in Scripture to such reliable, unchanging and trustworthy building blocks:

1. *God does not fail.*

   "Be strong and of a good courage, fear not, for the LORD thy God . . . will not fail, nor forsake thee" (Deuteronomy 31:6).

2. *God's Word does not fail.*

   "Not one of all the good promises the LORD your God gave you has failed" (Joshua 23:14, NIV).

3. *God's love and compassions do not fail.*

   "It is of the LORD'S mercy that we are not consumed, because His compassions fail not. They are new every morning: great is thy faithfulness" (Lamentations 3:22).

4. *What we do for God does not fail.*

   "But lay up for yourselves treasures in heaven, where neither moth nor rust doth corrupt" (Matthew 6:20).

5. *Faith does not fail.*

   "You are receiving the goal of your faith, the salvation of your soul" (1 Peter 1:9, NIV).

6. *The promise of eternal life will not fail.*

   "I give unto them eternal life; and they shall

never perish, neither shall any man pluck them out of my hand" (John 10:28).

7. *Love does not fail.*
"Love never fails. But . . . prophecies . . . tongues . . . knowledge . . . will pass away. And now these three remain: faith, hope and love. But the greatest of these is love" (1 Corinthians 13:8,13, NIV).

These building blocks can mean the difference between winning and losing at life.

DREAMS AND GOALS

If a person aims at nothing, he'll hit the target every time. A person is either going forward or backward — there's no such thing as a neutral stability. We need a clear path to follow.

Failure, for that reason, often lies not so much in defeat but in the lack of direction. Like goldfish, so many people keep going around and around in circles, zig-zagging in endless directional changes. Spend time with God, and learn to dream big dreams as you seek His will for your life.

Overcoming

God created us in His image. Throughout His-story, His less-than-perfect followers have left a legacy of overcoming incredible obstacles. Just "getting by" hardly seems what the Creator intended us to do.

A successful overcomer will learn to be tenacious in the pursuit of his goals. Those goals should be clearly defined and written down. Strategies may be modified, schedules may change, but the soon-to-be winner keeps his eyes on the prize. The dream of reaching the next goal fuels the fire. "Forgetting what is behind and straining toward what is ahead, I press on toward the goal to win the prize for which God has called me heavenward in Christ Jesus" (Philippians 3:13,14, NIV).

Non-overcomers, on the other hand, often resort to unrealistic fantasies. The successful person conceives a worthwhile purpose and envisions the possibility of might-be's and should-be's. Those clear-cut potentials generate the willpower for a person to say, "Here is what I must do to achieve my goals." Thus, such conceptions change a person from a frustrated dreamer into an inspired achiever.

GETTING STARTED

All God's children are far from perfect. We have pasts strewn with failures of various kinds. We are diamonds in the rough. Some are more polished and multifaceted than others, but all of us have an unfathomable amount of work still to be done.

No matter how defeated we are right now, however, we have the potential for success. Our greatest glory consists not in never failing, but in rising every time we do fail. It is not a disgrace to be defeated. Failing, and learning from errors, is probably one of the greatest (and least nurtured) talents in the world.

POWER PRINCIPLES

I can face my failures through a realistic examination of the causes — searching for solutions, not scapegoats.

I can release those failures through trusting in God's forgiveness and by forgiving those who may have helped initiate my defeats and failures.

I must rely on God to help me cope with the most bitter failures, always realizing He is more interested in my growth than in my comfort.

I can strengthen my healing from failure by reaching out to others in the midst of their defeats.

A POWER PROMISE

The thief [Satan, the author of failure] comes only in order that he may steal and may kill and may destroy. I came that they may have *and* enjoy life, and have it in abundance — to the full, till it overflows (John 10:10, AMP).

A PRAYER FOR POWER TO COPE WITH FAILURE

Father, receive my thanks for coming to give me abundant life and victory over defeat.

Help me to forgive those who may have caused my problems. Help me to be a bridge to others who have failed. Immerse me today in love and forgiveness and grace. Amen.

4

POWER TO COPE WITH IDENTITY PROBLEMS

Admittedly, the picture of George Washington on the back of the one-dollar bill looks rather staid and tense. Furthermore, in every painting or sketch made of the "Father of Our Country," he appeared to be either bad-tempered or unhappy. Actually, according to reports from his peers, the first Chief Executive of the United States was always insecure and ashamed of his wooden false teeth. Reflected on his face was the pain he felt — hardly the robust, courageous symbol he actually represented.

Abraham Lincoln had similar identity problems. For whatever reason — his rough-hewn childhood, a lack of formal education, his gangly appearance — he was extremely insecure when it came to personal relationships. Reportedly, when he asked his future wife to marry him, he turned his back and apologized for at least ten minutes because he was so awkward, inadequate and ill-equipped for such a commitment.

Johnny Carson, the "king of late-night television," once said, in effect, that he believed himself to be one of the most insecure people in America. "The insecurity heightens if I am ever in an elevator with other people," he said. "What am I ever going to say to these people?" Though he's great with prepared one-liners, he has trouble making impromptu small-talk.

Some of the most secure-appearing people have full-blown identity problems. Insecurity about one's self seems to be the great common denominator of all mankind. Many experience the same questions about "self" during the varied "passages" of life. The most absurd part of this common trait is that so many of us feel we face unique, uncommon, "special" identity problems.

We all have problems with knowing who we are and what we should be doing with our lives. It's always interesting to talk with individuals and ask what they dislike about themselves. A beautiful woman may grow red-faced over her teeth or freckles or eyebrows — things that most observers would never call detrimental. A polished, successful businessman, when asked about his weaknesses, may admit that he is disdainful of his big ears, receding hairline or "that extra fifteen pounds around my middle." Children, particularly teenagers, can produce a long list of weaknesses when asked. It's a commonality: All of us feel this way about ourselves in one form or another.

We go through life, too often feeling awkward, never quite fitting in, wondering if we're on the fringes and away from the "action," going into situations thinking that we are unwelcome intruders. These feelings are common to all age levels.

During recent years, additional identity problems have been highly publicized. Numerous magazine articles and television programs have targeted the housewife who says, "I'm tired of being some man's wife and several children's mother. I've gotta find out who I am." Likewise, the media searchlight has touched the "gray itch" phenomenon; men caught in mid-life identity crises have even been immortalized in songs and motion pictures such as *Middle-age Crazy.*

It seems that there's an explosion of identity problems, but the truth is this: The struggles have been around since mankind's first generation.

LESSONS FROM THE PAST

Nearly two thousand years ago, a man named Paul roamed the cities and dusty paths of the Mediterranean seacoasts. According to published reports, he came through the finest schools, was probably the brightest young man of his day, and was a proclaimed leader in the fight against the "brainwashing tactics" of the fastest growing "cults" of that generation.

But Paul (formerly known as Saul of Tarsus) met Jesus on the road to Damascus. His life was changed. Suddenly the "fair-haired boy" of the established religion became the despised "turncoat." Even after he was established as a leader of the Christians, he constantly faced challenges from all sides.

"All have forsaken me," Paul wrote to his young protégé (see 2 Timothy 4:10). Then he listed several people. Demas, Paul's close companion and associate evangelist, had gone back into the world; Alexander, the coppersmith, did him much wrong. Yet Paul could write, "Notwithstanding the Lord stood with me, and strengthened me" (2 Timothy 4:17). Here lies the real explanation of the paradox: God is all powerful in what He can do within a person.

There were those in Corinth, Philippi and other cities who kept tearing down the churches Paul had helped establish. It might have been easy for him to wonder whether anything was worth the effort and persecution.

Apparently, Paul also faced several physical handicaps. When he and Barnabas arrived in Asia Minor, the local people compared them to two ancient gods, one handsome (Barnabas) and one ugly (Paul). That sort of comparison must have been quite a blow to his self-esteem.

Some say that Paul had severe problems with his eyes. When he wrote to the church in Galatia, he added, "See what large writing I use." There were others who wrote down what he dictated. Certainly there is evidence that an eye problem caused Paul to have to bend over and look at the print. Paul admittedly had a "thorn in the flesh" that probably was never alleviated. But he could write nonetheless, "When I am weak, then am I strong" (2 Corinthians 12:10).

Paul faced the great contradiction: He boasted of God's unlimited power, yet he faced tremendous personal pain, anxiety, desperation, loneliness and changes for which he was ill-equipped. He was locked in a horrendous identity crisis. How did he cope with the problems? God!

WORD PICTURES

In the letters he wrote, Paul called himself and other Christians by many titles: believers, disciples, saints, children of God, citizens of heaven, the elect, the called ones. Likewise, Jesus had already given references to help establish our identity — light, salt, living stones, little children.

In the second letter to young Timothy, Paul used effective word pictures as symbols, models and illustrations to help Timothy understand who he was to be, likening the Christian to a soldier, an athlete, a farmer and a workman.

Timothy was obviously going through a difficult "passage" in his life. His father was not a Christian, so the spiritual conceptions in his life had come from his grandmother, Lois, and mother, Eunice. They had apparently wall-papered the rooms of his heart (and mind) with the Old Testament Scripture. When Paul came to Lystra, Timothy's home town, the young believer's heart burst into life. He became an astute follower of Christ, a companion to Paul and the pastor at Ephesus.

As Paul's protégé, Timothy apparently had difficulty with his identity, undoubtedly asking himself, *Why am I going through this? What's my role? What's my function? What's really important? Look at all the problems Paul is facing. Am I crazy to keep believing what we've been preaching?*

By reading Paul's letters to the young preacher, we can understand that Timothy was having trouble with himself. He was becoming ashamed of other Christians and was no longer comfortable with those friendships. He wasn't living up to his potential, and he was neglecting the reading of the Word of God. In fact, he was reaching a crisis state, feeling guilty and intimidated. In a phrase, Timothy was no longer the Christian believer Paul thought he should be.

Paul wrote, in effect, "I know that you're ashamed of me and my bonds. Come on, don't do this to me! Stir up the gift that is within you. Identify who you are and what your talents are, then maximize those. Get back into the Word and back to the basics. Stop being insecure. You are a young person. You are struggling. Be strong!"

The word pictures, then, were given to get Timothy back on track.

Soldier

> So you, my son, be strong — strengthened inwardly — in the grace (spiritual blessing) that is [to be found only] in Christ Jesus. And the [instructions] which you have heard from me, along with many witnesses, transmit *and* entrust (as a deposit) to reliable *and* faithful men who will be competent *and* qualified to teach others also. Take [with me] your share of the hardships *and* sufferings [which you are called to endure] as a good (first class) soldier of Christ Jesus. No soldier when in service gets entangled in the enterprises of [civilian] life; his aim is to satisfy *and* please the one who enlisted him (2 Timothy 2:1-4, AMP).

A good soldier, according to Paul, knows that he's chosen for duty and must be trained. He must submit the direction of his life to his commander. He must be disciplined and loyal. Without those elements, he becomes his own worst enemy.

In America, God has given us tremendous peace. We have seldom been attacked. Most young Americans will probably never face combat. However, when one travels to other countries, particularly to the Middle East, the contrast becomes quite stark.

In Israel, for example, upon graduation from secondary school, young men and women alike sign up for two years of military training. Their allegiance, love and commitment to their country are unparalleled in the world. They discipline themselves, not only for their personal survival, but for the loyalty they have to the state of Israel as well.

I was in the Holy Land recently and witnessed a number of young soldiers being inducted. Each had a rifle and a Bible. They pledged allegiance to the state of Israel and to Jehovah. An Israeli soldier told me, "We will train for years, possibly, for just fifteen minutes of combat!"

A good soldier is a deterrent, Paul was saying. He is trained, ready and always willing to serve. Paul was telling Timothy (and us) that God had selected him for a role. That role was to be a soldier of Jesus Christ, commissioned to the task of serving Him.

Athlete

The second word picture Paul used to help Timothy get back on track centers on athletics. "If any man strive for the mastery," Paul wrote, and the word he chose refers to an athlete.

The symbols of athletic competition in the New Testament ought to excite any person who is interested in sports. "Let us lay aside every weight . . . let us run with patience the race that is set before us, looking unto Jesus the author and finisher of our faith" (Hebrews 12:1,2). "Take off the sweatsuit," we're instructed, "and get on with the race!"

All of us run a race whether we know it or not. The Greek word for "race" is the word we use for stadium. We are in the arena, running (or walking) in competition against ourselves.

So Paul, in his word pictures, encouraged his young follower to be a disciplined runner, lest when he should compete in the race, he should be a castaway, or reject. "As I enter into the race," Paul explained, "I don't go in as a boxer who just beats the air. I am not there to play around. I have to go after the prize God is offering!" (see 1 Corinthians 9:24-27).

During Paul's time, the goal line for runners was a white pillar, a pole at the end of the stadium. All the runners gazed toward the pole. In the great games, the object was to run around and touch the pillar. The winner was given a crown, a wreath of wild olive branches. It was the symbol, the most significant sign of the consummate athlete and competitor.

"Looking unto Jesus," Paul wrote. He was dealing directly with Timothy's identity problems. "Don't look at your own weaknesses and failures," he exclaimed. "Don't fret over past traditions. Don't look at others. Don't worry about things over which you have little control. Just look to the Savior. Keep your eyes on Him. Look unto Jesus, the author and finisher of your faith."

If Christians want to fulfill their potential, they will be required to strive for mastery. The word *strive* means to agonize. Throughout the centuries, the athlete's threshold of pain has always determined his quality. The Olympic hopeful must agonize. How much pain can he handle? Can she go the extra two miles? Can he force himself to pump heavier iron? Can she swim one more lap? Can he do what no one else is willing to do?

Why should we think that the most glorious challenge in the universe — to be Christ's follower — would be any less agonizing? The Christian is called to strive for excellence. We cheapen that calling when we avoid discipline and pain.

The pivotal word in Paul's illustration about being an athlete is *if.* Frankly, Paul was pointing out a challenge, asking Timothy a loaded question. "If any man will follow Me," Jesus likewise challenged, "let him take up his cross."

"If any man will hear My voice, let him do what I say."
"If any man will hear the knock as I knock on the door."
"If any man will know the doctrine." The Scripture is
filled with that word of presupposition. "If any man
strive for the mastery . . . "

Farmer

The third word Paul used, "husbandman," relates to
an ancient agricultural term. A husbandman was a cul-
tivator, one who tilled the fields. In the Bible, the word
field has a double meaning. Many times the Lord referred
to a person's talent and gift in the same context. Paul
was writing on this basis. Plowing, planting, watering,
weeding, tending young plants, fighting the elements and
predators, and harvesting — these farming themes run
throughout the Bible. Yet why would Paul instruct Timothy
to be like a farmer? He was speaking on two levels. We
have our own personal farm that needs to be continually
cultivated. How we often hate that! It's difficult, denigrat-
ing work, requiring discipline. Then, of course, we have
the great field, the world, to which we must be responsible
in bringing the seed, joy and fruits of the gospel.

Workman

The last word picture Paul used to encourage Timothy
to keep on track is found in 2 Timothy 2:15: "Study to
shew thyself approved unto God, a workman that needeth
not to be ashamed, rightly dividing the word of truth."

In this sense, "workman" doesn't mean just doing
a job; it means applying one's self to the entire task — all
the work. The word Paul uses is very specific, and it is
a word for work that's inglorious, tough and wearisome.

Paul's word refers to a person doing the little things,

the slave tasks. One example would be working in a ship's galley — pulling the oars, chained to a rough board, rowing in time to some sweaty guy who was thumping on a drum, stuck on the bottom, no way to get out. No one giving credit. No one offering thanks. No one there to pat the workman's aching back. He would just be there, working away. Paul, through the inspiration of the Holy Spirit, told Timothy that he was to be that kind of workman. How deflating!

Having described the lowest sort of menial labor, Paul then had the audacity to say that we should not be ashamed of such a calling. The Greek word for ashamed means literally "insecure."

And the bottom line, according to the apostle, is that we be approved unto God. *Approved* translates "to come alongside of God." In other words, our purpose should be to respond as God calls us to His side, puts His arm around us and says, "You did well! I'm proud of you! You're so faithful!"

THE GOAL

Man's identity is largely tied to his hope. Hope erodes when there is no prospect for the future. That, in essence, reflects the identity crises men and women are facing today.

In the Bible, hope is always expressed in the context of the future — "a blessed hope," "hope beyond the grave." Everything relates to the future. But a lot of people have no hope because they have no future. Millions of people are searching today for direction, for an identity, for a purpose, for the peace that comes with hope.

Where do we find the ultimate solution to identity problems? In Jesus Himself.

Through Him also we have [our] access (entrance, introduction) by faith into this grace — state of God's favor — in which we [firmly and safely] stand. And let us rejoice *and* exult in our hope of experiencing *and* enjoying the glory of God. Moreover — let us also be full of joy now! Let us exult *and* triumph in our troubles *and* rejoice in our sufferings, knowing that pressure *and* affliction *and* hardship produce patient *and* unswerving endurance. And endurance (fortitude) develops maturity of character — that is, approved faith and tried integrity. And character [of this sort] produces [the habit of] joyful and confident hope of eternal salvation. Such hope never disappoints *or* deludes *or* shames us, for God's love has been poured out in our hearts through the Holy Spirit Who has been given to us (Romans 5:2-5, AMP).

We *can* live in the twentieth-century world without identity struggles. We can live unashamed, secure, strong and unafraid. God's favor is available, according to Paul, if we will function as disciplined soldiers, agonizing athletes, cultivating farmers and diligent workmen.

God doesn't desire to squash our self-esteem and personal identity, but He does want each life to be joined together into a great mosaic, creating a magnificent picture of total commitment to Christ.

"Who am I?" each of us asks. "Why am I here?" "What purpose do I have in life?" We are all, in one form or another, locked in an identity struggle. But Paul, in painting his word pictures, instructed us to get back to the basics, to get on track. Then he wrote, "You take what I am giving you, and you give it to others. Reproduce it. Share it. In the future, I expect you to duplicate what I am telling you now" (see 2 Timothy 2:2). The purpose and hope we have in Christ are transferable concepts, and in sharing God's design with others, we further establish our identity in Him.

Will it be easy? Paul hardly minced words when he referred to the diligence, agony, work and thankless tasks to which we are called. He truly lives, however, who has a work he can respect, a cause for which he would live and die, a faith that supports him in days of difficulty, great ideas and goals to prod him forward and hope to keep him company during the lonely hours.

It is the *process*, the *struggle*, that forms one's identity.

The Word of God says, "We are more than conquerors through him that loved us" (Romans 8:37). Our confidence, our identity, our strength, our hope — everything is in Him.

What, then, can threaten us? We must go forward as individuals under His banner, committed to a higher purpose, confident of His presence, our eyes on the prize. "Approved of God" — that is the answer for any person's identity problems.

POWER PRINCIPLES

I can face my identity problems through a realistic examination of my gifts and talents, realizing that God is interested in me — as an individual.

I can release my past personal problems through trusting in God's forgiveness, and by forgiving those who may have helped form my identity struggle.

I must rely on God to help me cope with the "Who am I?" and "Why am I here?" questions, always realizing He is more interested in my growth than in my comfort.

I can strengthen my healing from identity problems by reaching out to others in the midst of their struggles.

A POWER PROMISE

We are assured and know that [God being a partner in their labor] all things work together and are [fitting into a plan] for good to those who love God and are called according to [His] design and purpose (Romans 8:28, AMP).

A PRAYER FOR POWER TO COPE WITH IDENTITY PROBLEMS

Father, I know that I was brought into this world for a purpose. Nothing You do happens by accident.

Show me, I pray, Your purpose for my life. Help me to see that I can be most happy when I am reaching out to others. Therefore, help me to be Your hands to those around me. Amen.

5

POWER TO COPE
WITH SELF-DOUBTS

One of the more common, specific identity problems is that universal tendency to doubt. Self-criticism is as common as breathing. Few of us really like ourselves. Fewer still love ourselves. Yet Jesus was explicit when He said, "Love thy neighbour as thyself" (Mark 12:31). How can one love his neighbor unless he first loves himself?

Without self-love, it's almost impossible to get along with others. A person plagued with self-doubts may soon be overwhelmed by his own inadequacies.

THE CRIPPLING FACTOR

I have a friend (I'll call him Abner) who is rife with self-doubts. He appears just the opposite, however. He speaks forcefully. He always has a joke ready, and he delivers punch-lines with the finesse of Bob Hope. People accept him. He is well-liked socially and very successful professionally. Still, Abner uses his personality and mannerisms as giant cover-ups for his self-doubts. He cannot accept himself as he is, and he has failed to understand that people really do like him just as he is.

Self-doubting can be a painful problem. It's an ache that's hard to cure and even more difficult to define. On the one hand, the self-doubting person has an insatiable desire and need for affection, but he generally has an inability to receive and accept love. He is often insensitive to those who attempt to show him attention, yet resentful because no one seems to take a caring interest in him. The pattern of self-doubt often breeds self-pity, anger, bitterness and depression. Those traits often create an uneasiness around the self-doubter, which then complicates his problem. Others, especially those who also feel somewhat insecure, often withdraw from him. The inner struggle heightens. Finally, despair and suicide sometimes become "attractive" options.

God has faced this problem with mankind for centuries. He loves us, yet we turn away. We're insensitive to His desire to enter our lives. We act resentful at His intrusion, then we blame Him for our problems. It becomes a vicious cycle.

Self-doubt is the opposite of love, but it is also the opposite of faith, commitment and trust. Self-doubt is a crippling force, and the power to overcome its destructive tentacles must come from the Father of love and faith.

THE IMPORTANCE OF THOUGHTS

Solomon said, "As he thinketh in his heart, so is he" (Proverbs 23:7). Marcus Aurelius, an ancient philosopher, wrote, "A man's life is what his thoughts make of it." Ralph Waldo Emerson mused, "A man is what he thinks about all day long." Wise men and prophets throughout history have disagreed on nearly every major philosophical point, yet all great teachers have agreed that we are what we think about.

The heart (or inner self) is the center of one's view of himself. The heart decides, feels and thinks. Therefore, if a person wants to change his self-image, he must change his thoughts. That sort of transformation requires divine help. "Do not conform any longer to the pattern of this world, but be transformed by the renewing of your mind. Then you will be able to test and approve what God's will is — his good, pleasing and perfect will" (Romans 12:2, NIV).

To remove those destructive self-doubts, one must *accept the unchangeable* (success is not living without problems, but comes through realistically dealing with the difficulties), *achieve the possible* (conquering self-doubts always involves forward movement) and *acknowledge the inevitable* (God knows the end from the beginning — to refuse His design for our lives is senseless). Self-doubts will vanish as a man's thoughts center on God. The problem, then, is not doubting one's self, but doubting one's God.

THE NECESSITY OF FAITH

Doubt is an unpleasant experience. One of the Old Testament words for doubt means "to be up in the air, to be uncertain." God expects us to trust Him. He wants us to depend upon His sufficiency. He doesn't want us to doubt Him (though He knows we all will from time to time).

God did not flippantly create the universe. He didn't place the world in space as a mere habitat for mankind. He flung evidence of Himself throughout every molecule of creation so that we might understand and believe in Him. With such an array of proof available, no one has an excuse. Every man, woman and child has enough vivid truth to substantiate a faith in God the Creator.

But man often seems blind. He renounces the most obvious evidence, choosing instead man-made fantasies. The Bible points to doubt as deliberate, saying it is the renunciation of that which is obvious. "For the invisible things of him from the creation of the world are clearly seen, being understood by the things that are made, even his eternal power and Godhead; so that they are without excuse" (Romans 1:20).

No wonder Moses told the children of Israel, "God says that your problem is that you are a people of no faith" (see Deuteronomy 32:20). Jesus said the same thing to His disciples: "O ye of little faith!" (Matthew 6:30)

Faith is not the absence of information, not just a "leap in the dark." That would be senseless. Instead, God has provided much proof of Himself through creation, throughout recorded history and in the Bible. We have so much on which to build our faith.

Faith is based on confidence in God. Trust can overcome doubts. We can believe in Him for the "small" things — things like each breath of air, the changing seasons, the "good feeling" in worship and His willingness to cause us to grow into greater trust.

Accepting Jesus Christ as personal Savior is also hardly a "leap in the dark." Salvation's road is a well-worn path. Millions have already entrusted their lives to Christ. Many of the most well-known personalities have revealed how they have become "born again," telling in graphic detail how the Lord has changed their lives. With all the evidence pointing to the Christ of Calvary, it seems completely unnatural not to accept Him as Savior.

It may be suggested that Moses and Abraham (and

the other Old Testament heroes) had "leap-in-the-dark" faith (although the Bible plainly says that God spoke to them) since they had few prior experiences with God, no written Word and no one with whom to confirm God's voice. But in the twentieth century, considering the evidence, the easiest truth for mankind to accept should be the gospel of Jesus Christ. Why, then, are there still clouds of doubt?

Part of the answer is that distrust, rejection and self-imposed ignorance reign in the hearts of men and women. Professing Christians sometimes seem as guilty as nonbelievers. Things that are difficult to deal with often have a root of doubt: "Can I trust God? Can I believe Him?" Perhaps doubts cannot be dissolved until the question of faith is resolved.

The Bible describes several types of faith:

SPURIOUS — seeing the evidence, yet failing to yield (the demons tremble and have faith, but they have rejected God);

SHALLOW — having little growth;

SINCERE — doubting, yet believing; and

SAVING — putting God as the object of ultimate trust.

We all struggle with feelings of being tentative, hesitant, reserved, unsure and unstable, all of which are forms of doubt. When our "great expectations" are shattered and we're disappointed in life, often we become doubtful about the future. Still, we don't have to be spurious or shallow. God wants us to move from doubting into a mature faith.

The Foundation of Faith

"So then faith cometh by hearing, and hearing by

the word of God" (Romans 10:17). Faith grows through listening to credible words. That's true on both human and spiritual levels. If a husband doubts that his wife loves him yet she continually reinforces him with "I love you" phrases, he will soon allow the words to permeate his heart. Good words suppress doubt and raise confidence.

So it is with the Word of God. Jesus called the Word the *sperma*, the seed. The soil is the heart. Some soil is inhospitable. If the seed is thrown away or rejected, it isn't God's fault. It's the fault of the heart. The seed was neither negative nor ineffective. The response factor of the heart of man to God is all-important in bringing the seed to a harvest.

Therefore, the foundation of faith is God's Word. There can be little long-term faith without regular thirsting and hungering for the Bible. There are no champions of the Christian faith who haven't continually studied and immersed themselves in the Word of God. If you struggle with doubts about God and His goodness, one of the best pieces of advice I can give you is simply to commit yourself to the reading and study of the Bible, even when you don't seem to "get anything out of it." Give God's Word a chance to permeate your heart and mind. You'll find your doubts are steadily receding.

The Formulation of Faith

How does faith develop? It grows through personal acknowledgment and appropriation. The person who would have saving faith must state, "Not by my own righteousness."

Such self-renunciation is unwelcome news to modern man, particularly in America, where even the evangelical gospel is being meshed with the basic presupposition that we can polish ourselves through deliberate effort. In our own strength, we're told, we will be able to become what God wants us to be.

The Scripture, of course, strips us bare of such "logic." "There is none that doeth good, no, not one" (Romans 3:12). None can obey God by himself. "All have sinned and fallen short of the glory of God" (Romans 3:23). God doesn't want to destroy our hopes, but He does want to establish the ground rules. We in the flesh cannot please Him.

Paul, the sophisticated intellectual and strategist, said, "I am crucified with Christ: nevertheless I live; yet not I, but Christ liveth in me: and the life which I now live in the flesh I live by the faith of the Son of God, who loved me, and gave himself for me" (Galatians 2:20).

Faith is a *gift*. "By grace are ye saved through faith; and that not of yourselves: it is the gift of God" (Ephesians 2:8). Such a gift bankrupts pride and shatters doubt when the believer's confidence becomes firmly placed in the Lord. What a puzzling paradox!

The Flourishing of Faith

What is the benefit, the result, of faith? God's desire is that we should get control over our doubts, that we should never be intimidated, and that we should not walk around feeling inferior, shy and insecure. He wants us to become confident and faithful.

Jesus often spoke about trees. Good trees, He explained, have good fruit. The depth of the roots determines the quality and the size of the fruit. "By their fruits ye shall know them," He said (Matthew 7:20).

The fruit to which He referred is that which comes

from within. Fruit isn't merely attached to the outside. It comes, mysteriously, from deep inside. "For whatsoever is born of God overcometh the world: and this is the victory that overcometh the world, even our faith" (1 John 5:4). What world? This victory is for our personal world, the world of self-doubts. Then we can confront the economic world, the political world, the scientific world and the spiritual world in victory through faith in God.

Our faith becomes the indispensable element in removing self-doubts:

> But without faith it is impossible to please him: for he that cometh to God must believe that he is, and that he is a rewarder of them that diligently seek Him (Hebrews 11:6).

Faith assures success:

> Believe in the LORD your God, so shall ye be established; believe his prophets, so shall ye prosper (2 Chronicles 20:20).

Faith is essential in the Christian's walk:

> If any of you lack wisdom, let him ask of God, that giveth to all men liberally, and upbraideth not; and it shall be given him. But let him ask in faith, nothing wavering. For he that wavereth is like a wave of the sea driven with the wind and tossed (James 1:5,6).

Faith will breed love:

> And this is his commandment, That we should believe on the name of his Son Jesus Christ, and

love one another, as he gave us commandment (1 John 3:23).

Faith will bring peace and God's approval:

> Therefore being justified by faith, we have peace with God through our Lord Jesus Christ (Romans 5:1).

As Christians, we are to seek, address, confront and change the world in Christ's behalf. We are His servants reaching out to a hurting populace. If we are self-doubting cripples (emotionally or spiritually), we thwart God's plan.

Faith makes the difference. God's saving faith will grow into marvelous fruit, simultaneously killing doubt and bringing glory to God if we allow Him to fill our hearts.

The choice rests with us. What do we choose to think about — good or bad? Whom do we trust — God or self? To whose words do we listen — God's or man's?

> From the beginning God chose you to be saved through the sanctifying work of the Spirit and through belief in the truth. He called you to this through our gospel, that you might share in the glory of our Lord Jesus Christ. So then, brothers, stand firm and hold to the teachings we passed on to you (Thessalonians 2:13-15, NIV).

POWER PRINCIPLES

I can face my self-doubts through a realistic examination of my faults and needs, understanding that God is truly interested in me as an individual.

I can release my past self-doubts through trusting

in God's forgiveness, and by forgiving those who may have helped form my self-doubts.

I must rely on God to help me cope with my self-doubts and God-doubts, always realizing He is more interested in my growth than in my comfort.

I can strengthen my healing from self-doubts by reaching out to others in the midst of their struggles.

A POWER PROMISE

I have strength for all things in Christ Who empowers me — I am ready for anything and equal to anything through Him Who infuses inner strength into me, [that is, I am self-sufficient in Christ's sufficiency] (Philippians 4:13, AMP).

A PRAYER FOR POWER TO COPE WITH SELF-DOUBTS

Father, may the words of my mouth and the meditation of my heart be acceptable in Your sight, the only place where it really counts.

You are my Lord, my strength and my Redeemer.

I thank You for Him Who is the author and the finisher of my faith, and I wait for the culmination of my faith, which is the salvation of my soul.

Put Your blessing upon me, I pray, not because I deserve it, but because You promised it for this day, for Your glory and for my good. Amen.

6

POWER TO COPE
WITH STRESS &
FRUSTRATION

Twentieth-century Americans are a blessed people! We own 71 percent of the world's automobiles, 80 percent of the hospital beds, 82 percent of all the bathtubs, 52 percent of the high school students, 48 percent of all media/communications facilities, 60 percent of the life insurance policies, 34 percent of the meat and 33 percent of the world's railroads.

We have 140 doctors per each million people, as compared to 114 in England, 103 in New Zealand, 75 in France and only 4 in China.

The work time it takes to earn enough to buy something in the United States requires nearly twice as much time in England and ten times that amount in Soviet Russia. We have only 6 percent of the world's land and 7 percent of the globe's population, yet we have created almost half of the world's total wealth!

We have so much — too much, at times.

According to a just-released study by Emory University researcher Philip Hendrix, nearly 40 percent of Americans can be classified as "harried" — having too much to do, feeling rushed, trying to accomplish more than one thing at a time and feeling tremendously frustrated. "As we take on more roles, we have more demands on our time," says Hendrix, who is an associate professor of marketing at Emory's graduate school of business.

So much, it seems, has a price. In addition to leading the world in most areas of production and achievements, we also head many of the stress-related lists, from headaches to "burnout" to suicides.

For example, less than 10 percent of all headaches are actually injury- or illness-caused. Most are due to psychological factors: tension, stress and frustration. A headache is like a buzzer that signals a problem in our physical (or emotional) make-up.

In its extreme form, stress can lead to emotional deterioration, causing such symptoms as tiredness, cynicism, loss of motivation and a feeling of futility.

Many studies have been made on the causes and elimination of stress. Sadly, with the vicious cycle of today's world, few of those "cures" seem to have any lasting effect; perhaps we're too harried to take the time to properly use them.

SOME STRESS NEEDED

"It's impossible to lead a life without stress," says former Harvard Professor John Clarke. "But," he adds, "the management of stress is very much an achievable goal. What I attempt to show people in my lectures is how to bind stress rather than being bound by it."

This can be achieved, Clarke insists, by taking steps to change one's outlook on life. The first step involves looking deeply (and honestly) inside one's own self rather than blaming everything on outside forces.

Zig Ziglar often relates the story of the businessman who has an altercation with a traffic policeman while on his way to work. As a result, that businessman, fuming mad, rushes into his office and promptly barks at his secretary. She, in turn, gets mad at the salesman. Mr. Salesman eventually goes home and yells at his wife. The wife fusses at the child, and the child goes outside and kicks the cat. "So much time," Ziglar jokingly concludes, "could have been saved if the businessman would have just gone over to his salesman's house and kicked the cat!"

That, in a capsule, is an example of misdirected frustration that causes stress. Cain slew Abel not because he was angry at his brother, but because he had brought the wrong offering. He was being dishonest with himself. During the thousands of years since that murder, little has changed. The man who walks into a restaurant or bank and begins shooting people isn't angry at those particular people. He just explodes against convenient targets.

That's an extreme example, of course. Only a terribly sick person resorts to terrorism to vent his frustration and relieve his stress. But is it really any different when a man comes home feeling guilty from having an affair, then proceeds to berate his family for failing to live up to his expectations? Many divorces happen because the man or wife gets "fed up" with conditions at work. *Stress, unless controlled, eventually destroys.*

STRESS UNVENTED

Jake (not his real name), a highly competent music director in a large southern church, seemingly had everything going for him. He was lauded for his talent, and he had few peers when it came to motivating a choir or other musicians.

But Jake had experienced an unhappy marriage for twenty years. Simply put, he could not get along with his wife. During their marriage, he had avoided prolonged confrontations by immersing himself in his music. That worked well for some time, but when his children, seeing the problems at home, began to rebel, Jake was faced with a dilemma.

Sensing that he needed a close personal relationship, and resolving that he and his wife would never get along, he became very sympathetic with a woman in the church who was facing a similar situation in her own home. It didn't start as a sexual affair, but the friendship soon blossomed into a full-blown, illicit liaison.

The stress that he had been experiencing with a bad marriage was now compounded by the guilt he was feeling, but he refused to face the original problem. Eventually, after the affair became public knowledge, he resigned from his position with the church.

Jake and his lover eventually separated, and both went back to their mates. From that point, the similarities greatly differ. The woman entered a time of counseling. Soon she was joined by her husband, and the marriage vows were renewed.

Jake, on the other hand, still refused to deal with his problem. More than once, as he and I talked candidly, Jake merely shrugged off the suggestion that he needed to work out a livable relationship with his wife. "We've been this way since we got married," he said nonchalantly. "I don't think there's anything that can be done."

He had resigned himself to the situation, though his wife began counseling. The fighting had stopped and the verbal fireworks no longer went off, but both of them were emotional time-bombs.

Jake's talent was almost limitless, so he didn't cease being productive. His failing there, however, was that he didn't calculate the toll that his stress would take. A year later, Jake died from a heart attack.

Not all stories are as serious as Jake's, but no one lives today without stress. There are methods and guidelines, however, for dealing with the frustrations we all face.

CONTROLLING STRESS

There are many simple, everyday tips for coping with stress. The following list (borrowed from many of the stress-reduction experts) can provide the beginning steps in conquering this gigantic foe.

1. *Home life.* We seem to always hurt most the ones we love, and if left uncorrected, the guilts and frustrations that fester as a result can become vicious cycles.

Instead of letting that happen, it is extremely important to form lasting relationships at home with one's family. A lasting love bond involves both "little things" (a walk in the forest with one's teenager, a verbal "pat on the head" given at the proper moment, a surprise "thank you" card) and "big things" (gifts, vacations together, candlelight dinners) that cement relationships and build strongholds against stressful outside pressures.

2. *Planning.* One of the best ways to reduce stress comes through mapping one's strategy ahead of time, allowing for interruptions and last-minute changes, and refusing to lose control.

Almost all stress-reduction experts teach their students to start every day correctly by organizing details and thoughts the night before — for instance picking out the clothes to be worn the next morning. "Otherwise," one teacher says, "you set yourself up for stress by starting your day in a big rush."

Moreover, it's important to set short-, medium- and long-range goals. Time management has become a science, yet so few of us will admit we need help in this area.

Confusion creates the basis for frustration, but an ordered life definitely limits stress.

3. *Love.* It is important to show our deepest emotions to loved ones, and that category is certainly not limited to family members. Each of us needs to have friends with whom we share our dreams, hurts and thoughts. Given the chance, there are many people who are more than willing to return our love and who also want to talk about their feelings, problems and anxieties.

The worst possible alternative is bottling up our thoughts and worries. This almost always triggers stress. In fact, there is nothing wrong with crying on someone's shoulder. (Scientific research has shown that a good cry can greatly relieve tress.)

4. *Relaxation.* Being single-minded (having only one major activity or interest) tends to build stress. Conversely, stress reduction often starts when a person finds a relaxing outside interest — a hobby, a project, a sport or an academic pursuit. This interest, by the way, should not center on inactivity (such as watching television, movies or spectator events), but should involve active participation.

5. *Habits.* Some unconscious routines, though small in nature, become collective stress factors. For example, while driving to work, what a person listens to on the radio can alter his behavior. Psychological studies have proved that loud, pulsating music played in the car causes

stress. Experts suggest setting the dial on a station that features soft, relaxing melodies. Another alternative would be listening to a positive motivation cassette tape.

Impatiently punching and repunching elevator buttons, tapping one's fingers on the desk while waiting for a meeting, angrily and absentmindedly tensing one's muscles — all these are collective stress builders that can turn a person into the proverbial bundle of nerves.

Instead of wallowing in the frustrating events of the day, it's important to take moments to think pleasant thoughts, inhale deeply, clear the mind and relax those muscles. Pacing one's self is a carefully calculated talent performed by the wise.

6. *Listening.* Stress often builds when a person, any person, focuses too much on his own problems. In a world that seldom encourages communication, it is essential to listen to what others are saying.

Often we expect too much of others; then, when they let us down, our disappointment adds to our already heavy stress load, especially if that person is a friend, mate or child whom we love. But when we learn to listen to (and really hear) others, we recognize that they have difficulties, too, and those factors could be the reason they let us down.

7. *Personal life.* The body is a temple, the shrine of one's soul and the home for a person's heart. To reduce stress, we must be careful not to abuse that body, to get proper rest, to exercise regularly and to have a balanced, nutritional diet.

One often-overlooked contributor to stress is that we sometimes sacrifice our own health for the sake of helping others. Actually, there's nothing wrong with being somewhat selfish about one's time. Even Jesus had to get away by Himself on occasion.

One should even pamper himself every once in a while with a gift (though it certainly doesn't have to be expensive) or with an evening all alone to reflect. Self-gifts like these will help build self-esteem and relieve stress.

8. *Attitude.* The worst possible thing to do is give up hope. Researchers have shown, almost conclusively, that the loss of hope greatly contributes to stress. The person who is pessimistic about life in general will feel that he has no control over the events in his life. The person who intends to cope with stress must therefore cultivate an optimistic attitude.

"Count your blessings, Name them one by one," the song suggests. That idea remains thoroughly modern mental medicine. Simply by adding up the positives in life (family, spouse, job, good health, church, opportunities) can help us become cheerful. A "count your blessings" perspective helps us see how thrilling life can really be.

9. *Spiritual life.* Though this factor is listed last, it is first in importance. One's personal relationship with God is the guideline that stress-reduction experts often leave out. But without God, there can be no lasting peace. Time spent in prayer, worship and renewal will help restore one's soul and relieve bodily stress. God's power and sustaining strength take away harmful stress.

HASSLES AND HELP

Richard S. Lazarus of the University of California at Berkeley recently conducted a study on the correlation between stress and health. His conclusion (as reported in *Psychology Today*): "We should be cautious in generalizing from our results. But we do feel we have demonstrated that the small defeats and troubles of our daily lives may cause as much harm as the great ones."[1]

Hassles, we all agree, are a part of daily life — "the little foxes, that spoil the vines" (Song of Solomon 2:15). It's the little hassles that really spoil life. Everyone's tolerance and reaction to such annoyances differ widely. Yet there are common reflexes. When pressure is high (as it always seems to be), the smallest frustration creates bigger problems. The more frequent and intense the hassles, the poorer one's overall mental and physical health becomes.

The power to cope with stress and frustration one day at a time becomes increasingly important. Equally monumental is the advice given thousands of years ago by King David, the leader of an entire nation:

> Don't get so upset because of all that goes wrong
> . . . trust in the Lord and do what's right . . . get
> great joy in relying on God . . . He will give you
> the desires of your heart. Commit yourself to the
> Lord, trust in Him and He will bring it to pass
> (Psalm 37:1, 3-5, Author's paraphrase).

The choice, it seems, is clearly up to each of us. Will we let the little things build up to a point of explosion, or will we develop good, stress-reducing habits?

POWER PRINCIPLES

I can face stress and frustration through a realistic examination of the causes, remembering that nothing happens in isolation, whether people or problems are the source of my stress.

I can release my stress through trusting in God's forgiveness, and by forgiving those who may have contributed to the frustrations I feel.

I must rely on God to help me cope with stress, always realizing He is more interested in my growth than in my comfort.

I am strengthened and healed from the harmful effects of stress by reaching out and understanding others in the midst of their frustrations.

A POWER PROMISE

And the peace of God, which transcends all understanding, will guard your hearts and your minds in Christ Jesus (Philippians 4:7, NIV).

A PRAYER FOR POWER TO COPE WITH STRESS AND FRUSTRATION

God, I need Your help to cope with stress. Forgive me for ignoring Your peace.

Thank You for caring enough to be with me even through the worst of times, and for taking away the ill effects of my stress-filled world.

Most of all, help me to seek You, whom to know is life and peace and health. Amen.

7

POWER TO COPE WITH CAREER UNCERTAINTIES

A passer-by came upon a construction site. Seeing several men working, he asked one sweaty chap what he was doing.

"I'm mixing mortar for the bricks," the worker replied nonchalantly.

To another, the inquirer asked, "What are you doing?"

Though he was also mixing mortar much in the same manner as the first man, the second worker mused, "I'm just helping to put this building up."

Leaving the first two men, the spectator walked to another man doing a similar task.

"What are you doing?" he said.

The third worker looked up, his mind dancing with thoughts of blueprints and drawings. "I'm helping to build a cathedral with a spire that reaches to the sky," he answered enthusiastically, "and soon hundreds of people will be worshiping within these walls!"

All three workers were performing similar tasks, but each one was doing his job with a different perspective.

In today's high-tech world (and increasingly so, according to the popular book *Megatrends*), man's *perspective* on his work becomes supremely important.

We live in a highly transient society, and it's not uncommon for a worker to change jobs every two to three years. Especially in America's urban areas, long-term employment with the same corporation is a rarity anymore.

UPWARD MOBILITY

Few societies in the world provide the same avenues as America for "climbing the ladder." Magazines such as *Savvy, Inc., Money, Success* and *Forbes* focus on the men and women who have proved that a person can indeed reach seemingly limitless plateaus.

Free enterprise exists similarly in only a handful of other countries. A street sweeper in Leningrad knows that he will probably always be a street sweeper. A grain farmer in one of the Indian states has little hope of rising higher either in vocation or in caste. Even in free areas of Europe and South America, many limitations exist to dampen the entrepreneurial spirit.

Not in America. Here, the second son of small-town, church-going, flag-waving parents from the Illinois prairie was able to become the voice for the leading mid-America radio station, spend thirty-three years as one of the best-known Tinseltown stars and eventually become both the Governor of California and President of the United States.

But therein is the twist. In a society that offers, even applauds, upward mobility for its citizenry, many are caught in the battle of "great expectations." Children are pushed to join the Little League and cheerleading squads. Teenagers are often forced into career decisions based more on hope than fact. Going to *the* university and pledging *the* fraternity or sorority sometimes take precedence over what should be the best reason for attending college. Once in the corporate world, would-be leaders often must learn quickly to manipulate, sidestep and back-stab in order to succeed (or so suggest a number of best-selling books).

Mothers are often deprecated for making the wise choice to stay at home and devote precious years to rearing children. Such a person who dares refuse to join the corporate climb may be labeled "nonmotivated."

The problem lies in expectations. Quite frankly, some people are not able (or do not want) to move on to higher levels of achievement. Likewise, some people (who would be ill-advised to face the rigors of upward mobility) are falsely stimulated by the glorious picture of top-level "success."

It's not wrong for a person to work on an assembly line, collect money at the public parking lot or clean motel rooms. The waitress, the barber and the hired farm hand all perform a valuable service to mankind. That person may never become the boss or owner (and may not want such responsibility), but he (or she) can be proud of being the best at whatever he chooses to do and of giving a day's labor for a day's pay.

Not everyone can go from being a secretary or receptionist to carrying that $400 leather briefcase into his (or her) "Senior Vice President" suite. For many people, such a goal is unrealistic. Not everyone possesses that kind of experience, ability, mobility, time or desire. Furthermore, it would be a strange world for everyone to actually reach the top levels. That proverbial "all chiefs and no Indians" society would soon crumble.

God has given inborn gifts, abilities and talents. There is nothing wrong with being blessed with a great number of talents; however, one's worth is not lessened by having fewer gifts (as long as that person performs to the fullest).

> For the kingdom of heaven is as a man travelling into a far country, who called his own servants, and delivered unto them his goods. And unto one he gave five talents, to another two, and to another one; to every man according to his several ability; and straightway took his journey (Matthew 25:14,15).

Why would Jesus address the topic of talents? In telling the parable, was the Savior alluding to a principle of job discrimination? No. He was teaching His followers the needed lesson of being faithful with whatever we're given in life. A sense of personal worth and fulfillment must hinge on what a person does with his talents. As such, success doesn't always rest on the next higher rung of the corporate ladder despite the popular notion that happiness always involves that which is bigger, better, more expensive, higher and greater in the public spotlight.

While most of the world is concerned with day-to-day survival, Americans seem more worried about the perks of the next higher position and whether the new job will provide a salary large enough to afford that shiny new car with power windows, lumbar support seats and an electronic cigarette lighter.

Taken to the extreme, our insatiable desire for upward mobility creates more wants, and those wants often flood our lives with new levels of unhappiness, frustration and inadequacy. We find ourselves unable to cope with the knowledge that we cannot comfortably buy our sixteen-year-old a brand-new, low-slung sports car for his birthday; that our teenager may actually have to participate in paying for his college education; or that the house we live in has less square footage than the others on the block.

REACHING

But what about upward mobility? Is there nothing to be said for "pulling myself up by my own bootstraps"? What about the "Great American Dream" of each individual's reaching for his own "manifest destiny"? The semantics create a real tension, especially for the Christian who also wants to include God's will in that string of career choices. Perhaps no other verse in the Bible touches the subject like Matthew 6:33: "But seek for (aim at and strive after) first of all His kingdom, and His righteousness (His way of doing and being right), and then all these things taken together will be given you besides"(AMP).

How high can a person strive and reach? That is clearly up to each individual to determine. A person who works in a mill doesn't necessarily want to own his own mill. Some people will do a better job working from nine to five. The person who aspires to run his own business may find that the business owns him! The owner must surrender a certain amount of time and freedom to attain that "enviable" position.

Climbing the corporate ladder or owning one's own business is certainly not wrong. America has reached greatness largely because of entrepreneurs. But being content at doing a "menial" task is no less wrong. There's a place for both. Neither the janitor nor the president of a company should disdain the other. Both are needed.

GUIDELINES

Since all levels of achievement are acceptable, how does one know what career options to choose? For the Christian, God will make His way known through a careful study of His Word. As we seek to abide in Him, He plants the seeds of His will in us. He uses our conscience to guide, though the undisciplined conscience can be unreliable. He also uses circumstances, and, according to Colossians 3:15, He uses the conviction of the Holy Spirit: "Let the peace of Christ rule in your hearts, since as members of one body you were called to peace. And be thankful" (NIV). That kind of peace comes only through the Holy Spirit's nurture.

To know God's will concerning career choices, it is helpful if one is in good physical, mental and spiritual condition, and that one be maturing (1 Corinthians 13:11). God's will comes to those who are yielded (Romans 12:1), who desire to know His will (John 7:17,18), who daily seek to serve Him (Matthew 6:24), who accept His authority (Luke 6:46), who have faith (Hebrews 11:6), who pray and wait (James 1:5,6), and who have learned to distinguish between good and evil (Hebrews 5:14).

A balance is needed. Too often career choices are made merely because of a desire for greater wants. Material satisfaction may be a by-product of one's labor, but it should never be the ultimate goal. Selfish wants often exalt an inflated opinion of self, and they usually cover up (temporarily) spiritual hunger and thirst. Motives that endanger the divine principles of temperance, self-control, humility and godliness must never be allowed to dominate the Christian's decision-making process.

The same guidelines apply for a young person deciding on a life's work, for a college graduate trying to determine the next career step, for a mother of four who is torn between home and career and for the fifty-six-year-old who must make a critical "upward mobility" decision. "The steps of a good man are ordered by the LORD: and he delighteth in his way" (Psalm 37:23).

CONFLICTS

If a career choice were a one-time decision, life might be more simple. The choices come often, however, and conflicts are often a part of working.

The first reaction to an unexpected crisis — whether it's a new boss or a difficult co-worker situation — is usually this: "Why did this happen? Why to me? And why now of all times?" No trouble is timed well. Conflicts usually occur at the worst possible moments, often simultaneous with other problems at home, at church or someplace else in our lives. We never seem prepared for such troubles, so the problems stun and intrude into our lives at the same time.

The apostle Peter had many unworkable career situations. He seemed to be the most human of all the disciples. He always spoke before thinking, and then would reap the stinging results. He wasn't the most reliable. Still, in 1 Peter 4:12, he advised us how to cope with conflicts:

> Beloved, do not be amazed *and* bewildered at the fiery ordeal which is taking place to test your quality, as though something strange — unusual and alien to you and your position — were befalling you (AMP).

We shouldn't think it strange when trouble comes; we're human beings. The world contains a lot of people with a lot of problems. Failing is common to all. We should even be grateful, because trouble makes us aware of God's presence. The outcome will show God's purpose, and that will bring greater happiness.

Likewise, all of us should take comfort in the fact that no one is alone in his troubles. Others share equally in the pain when there are conflicts at work. The boss who makes unpopular decisions may be suffering far beyond his disgruntled workers.

The person with a long-term career in mind will understand that conflicts often result in greater maturity. Overcoming trouble makes a person stronger; it firms up emotional and spiritual muscles. Coping with conflicts will lay a foundation for future challenges, enabling a person to deal with problems from strength and not weakness. "And the God of all grace, who called you to his eternal glory in Christ, after you have suffered a little while, will himself restore you and make you strong, firm and steadfast" (1 Peter 5:10, NIV).

WORK MONOTONY

Can work be meaningful during an entire career? Is that work a source of fulfillment, or is it just something to do for forty-five years so that a person can afford vacations and hobbies? Is work a punishment, or can it truly be a pleasure?

Part of the problem with most work is that at least some of the time, it's boring and dull. Most people do the same things over and over again — pushing buttons, turning spindles, spinning computer disks, driving endless miles. Even a person with an "exciting" job — a race car driver like Richard Petty or an actor like Charlton Heston — must repeat the same tasks again and again to remain successful.

Some inspiration may come from the fact that even certain creative work has a boring aspect to it. The painter's brush strokes, the construction worker's hammer thrusts and the writer's plotting of a novel, for example, all function much the same way each time. There's a certain sense in which no work, no matter how glamorous or well-paid, is free from drudgery.

Here are several thoughts to help offset the dull moments. First, one should remember that he is not the only one with frustrations. Work is a threat to the natural laziness of mankind, but work is good for each of us. Man resents making an effort when he doesn't feel self-interests are at stake. Actually, they always are, whether we like it or not. Work brings fulfillment and meaning. Work brings self-worth and a livelihood.

Second, one should realize the freedom that's at stake. The struggle of the immigrant workers to choose and share in the benefits of labor should inspire Americans. We take so much for granted. Quality, not boredom, should be our constant companion.

We can also reflect on a greater purpose than the actual work. A mother who's helping put her children through college, a dad who's holding a family together, a single parent who's raising a child and planning a future — all these are tremendous, nonmonotonous challenges.

Finally, we can recapture the side benefits of work — providing for our families, meeting other people, sharing in friendships with other employees, supporting the success of one's company and nation, and reaping the joy of health through activity. Unemployment, on the other hand, is seldom fun or beneficial.

CHANGES

But what happens when the plant closes down, leaving a person unemployed? Or, as so often happens of late, what does a forty-six-year-old man do when he walks into the company for which he has worked for twenty years and is met with the note, "We regret to inform you that due to a change in our corporate structure, you will no longer be needed in our employment." What then?

The yellow light at an intersection isn't an invitation to proceed wildly but signals caution and safety. Red lights bring order to what would otherwise be chaos. And changes, like the varying colors of traffic signs, will always play a large role in our lives. A person who lives without change often finds that the only difference between a rut and a grave is the length.

When changes come, the successful person faces reality, admits failure (if needed) and moves forward toward growth, maturity and new challenges. The following are thoughts relating to career changes. At an "intersection," one must define goals clearly and specifically, asking, "Where do I want to go now? What do I want to do with my life? Do I have time and the wherewithal to do that one thing I've never been able to do — go to college, volunteer for a service organization, move to a farm?"

A person then must develop a plan to proceed to that goal, refining and reworking it as necessary, but keeping the ultimate goal in mind at all times. Many career counselors are available to help a person reach his new goals. And the Christian has the Master Career Counselor to help and guide. The truly successful person has committed his life to Him. This is so simple, but so often overlooked. "Commit thy works unto the LORD, and thy thoughts shall be established" (Proverbs 16:3).

POTENTIAL

Many inspirational speakers, myself included, have often used the uplifting message, "You can become whatever you want to be!" Though the phrase sounds wonderful, life can be a painful teacher in quite another direction. All people, despite Thomas Jefferson's prose, are not truly equal. Each of us has unique gifts and talents (and varying amounts of the same), but nobody can merely decide to be whatever he wants to be. We're limited to some extent by our native capacities and abilities.

Almost every young boy wants to grow up and be a heralded quarterback, and nearly every ten-year-old girl has aspirations to be a fashion model or movie star. But as we know, not everyone has Dan Marino's arm or Cheryl Tiegs's perfect face. Much can be said for intense training and development, but raw talent is also important.

We can all become "more," but never more than our inner potential. There's no comparison between self-realization and the world's idea of "success." Becoming all we can be, which should be everyone's desire, is quite different from becoming whatever we want to be. Only the individual and God can truly know what one's inner potential might be. Career decisions must come from that growing knowledge.

POWER PRINCIPLES

I can face career insecurities, decisions, changes and monotonies through a realistic examination of my God-given talents and desires, remembering that my steps are ordered by the Lord when I am seeking His will.

I can release my career problems through trusting in God's guidance and forgiveness, and by forgiving those who may have contributed to the insecurities and frustrations I feel.

I must rely on God to help me cope with career changes, always realizing He is more interested in my growth than in my comfort.

I can strengthen my coping power by reaching out to others in the midst of their career struggles.

A POWER PROMISE

Trust in the LORD with all thine heart;
and lean not unto thine own understanding.
In all thy ways acknowledge him, and he shall
direct thy paths (Proverbs 3:5,6).

A PRAYER FOR POWER TO COPE
WITH CAREER INSECURITIES

God, please be with me through the decisions I make. Forgive me for rejecting You at so many crossroads of my life.

Thank You for caring enough to guide me and work through me. Help me to reflect Your love and concern to those around whom I work, even during the tense times and career changes. May my co-workers see You through me. Amen.

8

POWER TO COPE WITH CRITICISM

"SUPPORT BARRIER-FREE DESIGN," the bumper sticker pronounced. I wondered what the saying meant; then I noticed the license plate — it was marked "Handicapped." The concept was clear. Building designs have always been next to impossible for those with certain physical impairments. The bumper sticker supported a change in awareness concerning the construction of steep inclines, steps, doors, restroom facilities and access areas of all kinds.

Moves to acquaint the public with the special problems of the handicapped are working. Today, all new building codes require barrier-free designs. Discrimination against the handicapped sector of society is waning.

"Support barrier-free design" is also an apt slogan for other areas of life. Not all barriers are physical. Some of the greatest obstacles are critical words.

PIERCING WORDS

Mankind seems to have an innate ability to criticize. Children, because they lack tact, can sometimes be more cruel than adults, making fun of a person's physical abnormality or picking on an especially weak playmate. What parent has not cringed in horror as his "darling" son or daughter asked loudly about a bypasser's physical differences?

By the teenage years, fault-finding becomes a bona fide science. Collegians are adept at developing criticism to new levels, primarily because those years are times of great questioning and skepticism. Adults are no different, especially when the reproofs are directed at the craziness of "that younger generation." And by the "golden years," criticizing and analyzing are so second-nature that the barbs can be tossed with merely a nod or a knowing smile.

THE OTHER SIDE OF THE COIN

But what happens when criticism is leveled at us? "With all due respect," the well-meaning person begins, and then he proceeds to point out our glaring errors.

"Can I be honest with you?" another friend asks. Then without bothering to listen for a reply, he lists something he doesn't like.

"I don't want to be critical, but . . . "

Usually the personal analysis comes from a close friend who feels that his ideas are justified, or perhaps he feels an obligation, for business or personal reasons, to set the record straight.

Criticism almost always triggers an instant response, and resentment immediately sets in. Our guard naturally goes up, and we begin thinking of our best defense.

We all have a basic need to be accepted and praised, so critical remarks become piercing threats. They cannot be laughed at or shrugged off. Criticism universally creates personal pain, with the most painful being that which is directed toward the individual rather than his actions. "You stupid jerk," we exclaim disdainfully at a co-worker, "why can't you ever do anything right?" "You always burn the potatoes," a husband yells at his wife rather than remarking that the potatoes taste burned. The problem may have been the pan. Regardless, focusing on the person only increases the trauma.

RESULTS

If all fault-finding were justified, perhaps it would be easier to accept. It is said that learning from constructive criticism can be a tremendous stepping stone to success. But most remarks aren't justified (or the situation may become so muddied that the reason for the remark no longer matters). When that is the case, anger comes quickly. We get "boiling mad." We enjoy hurling verbal abuse back at our "attacker." The Bible describes such reciprocal slander as "tongues that are like swords" (see Psalm 64:2,3).

Anger, when expressed in slicing sarcasms, brings more hurt. Taken to the extreme, such anger is a killer, a smoldering volcano. Many murders and other forms of physical violence have come about as a result of seemingly harmless words.

No one enjoys being picked on. The stings of criticism cut to the soul. The person who first said "Sticks and stones may break my bones, but words will never harm me" had a rose-colored view of life. Words hurt much deeper than "sticks and stones."

REACTIONS

How can a person cope with criticism — either positive or negative? The first step is to make a quick evaluation, not react with instant indignation. Unfortunately, our emotions usually rush ahead of logic and reason. But we need to stop and ask whether the remarks are justified. If they are, then admitting the mistake in the wake of valid criticism stops the other person quickly, often leading him to understand and make allowances. Other factors may come to light at a later time that may soften the mistake, and that makes one's fast apology look even better.

On the other hand, are the remarks unjustified and totally out of order? If so, then a speedy evaluation can be followed by a confrontation with the accuser. Why should a person "stew" for hours and days? Once the facts are sorted from fiction, there's nothing wrong with a cool-headed and honest encounter. To accept truly unjustified slander gives falsehood a victory, and such nonaction not only compromises one's character, but the words left unsaid may also entrench evil thoughts that can grow into violence. Meeting untrue criticism makes other people hesitant to level such false remarks toward a person again.

Quick evaluation and a speedy, honest response — not instant indignation — those are the keys to coping with criticism. "Be ye angry, and sin not" (Ephesians 4:26), we're told. Standing up for what's right is not only justified, but extremely important as well. The instruction is for us to never lose control or return the same person-centered verbal abuse that we received.

A BETTER WAY

Personal criticism is not God's style. He hates sin, but He loves the sinner. He forgives our imperfections.

That perspective sheds new light on coping with criticism.

Love is God's starting point. Our problem is that we're often centered on our humanness. One of my favorite posters says, "To err is human — I am uncomfortable around gods." Blundering doesn't imply that a person is bad, just that he's imperfect.

Nobody is perfect; therefore, no one has cause to resent or resist true correction. All of us, Paul said, have sinned and fallen short of the glory of God. If we're in error, therefore, we should accept correction and act likewise.

COMMUNICATION

The opposite of criticism isn't silence; it's truth spoken in love.

> Rather, let our lives lovingly express truth in all things — speaking truly, dealing truly, living truly. Enfolded in love, let us grow up in every way *and* in all things into Him, Who is the Head, [even] Christ, the Messiah, the Anointed One (Ephesians 4:15 AMP).

Uncritical relationships are generally based less on those things about which two people agree than on *how* they agree. If we learn to be uncritical toward others, our ability to cope with criticism will come easier.

Here are some communication guidelines that can help form the basis for an uncritical posture. First, it's important to avoid making (or listening to) unkind remarks about others. Even "lampooning" or joking about others often comes at another's hurtful expense. This first step seems so simple; few, however, are able to conquer that insatiable desire to gossip.

Second, we shouldn't attach the worst interpretation to what we see in others. We don't know the complete story. What is seen may be totally misleading.

When speaking or listening, truth must be paramount. Believing a lie is frightening, but telling a lie is devastating. Even "white" lies and half-truths can shatter lives.

We should never expect perfection in others. God alone is perfect. We don't have to tolerate deception, compromise our convictions or accept negligence, but we still have no right to expect perfection in those around us.

Why waste our energies on worthless activities, especially by lashing out and reacting to criticism? What we do in life should have a lasting quality to it; slander hardly fits that category. It's sad that long-term relationships often are sacrificed for the savory, short-term taste of criticism.

Beyond that, we should never neglect to encourage others. Both children and adults need constant affirmation and recognition. The successful person realizes those universal needs and builds on them. The attention one gives to others creates in them a flow of energizing life.

CHOICES

One should always remember that mankind was made in God's image. We are whole: body, mind (soul) and spirit. Disharmony, impurity and intemperance in any of our being will contaminate everything else.

In that light, remember that we have a choice. We can cope with criticism in a short-term manner by slinging slanderous remarks back at the accuser. Unfortunately, no one wins with such reactionary methods. Or we can choose the long-term answer, which means a realistic examination of the criticism, then swift, appropriate action.

God does give us power to cope with criticism as we seek to preserve dignity, harmony and integrity.

> Kind words do not cost much. They never blister the tongue or lips. Though they do not cost much, they accomplish much. They make other people good-natured. They also produce their own image in other men's souls, and a beautiful image it is.
>
> — Pascal

POWER PRINCIPLES

I can cope with criticism through an honest evaluation of the remarks, especially as I ask God for cool-headed wisdom.

I can release the stinging hurt of such criticisms by trusting in God's guidance and forgiveness, and by forgiving those who have slandered me.

I must rely on God to help me cope with both justified and unjustified criticisms, always realizing He is more interested in my growth than in my comfort.

I can strengthen my power to cope with criticism by sharing good words, not just desiring kind accolades, reaching out to others who are in the midst of the hurt that caused them to criticize.

A POWER PROMISE

> Pleasant words are as honeycomb, sweet to the mind and healing to the body (Proverbs 16:24, AMP).

A PRAYER FOR POWER TO COPE
WITH CRITICISM

Father, help me to understand that power which lies resident in my mouth. Help me to grasp the fact that I have the ability to give life or death through my choice of words.

Remind me each day that kind words cost nothing, but harsh words can devastate people.

Therefore, Lord, give me the wisdom needed to better comprehend criticism when it comes my way. If it is needed, help me to heed correction. If it is unjustified, provide me with the proper words to defuse an uncomfortable and tense confrontation.

Help me to remember to speak and react as You did when You walked on earth as a man — with strength, love, honor and truthfulness. Amen.

9

POWER TO COPE WITH LONELINESS

One summer a little boy named Jimmy spent a week away from home at a camp for the very first time. A typical eleven-year-old, he wasn't much of a letter writer, but on Wednesday of that week, his parents received a hastily scrawled postcard from him.

> Dear Mom and Dad,
>   There are fifty boys here this week at camp. I sure wish there were only forty-nine.
>
> Jimmy

What child, teenager, adult or elderly person has not experienced (or doesn't continue to feel) that utter despair at being alone and lonely? It's an all-encompassing emotion that can overtake anyone at almost any time. An unfamiliar airport or motel, a new school on the first day, a church where everyone else seems to know everyone else, a party where attempts to mingle only produce casual glances, that employment office where no one seems interested in helping, a class reunion — all are examples of moments when a person is gripped with uncomfortable, fear-producing loneliness.

Feeling alone and separated from others is hardly just a twentieth-century emotion. Literature through the ages has been filled with reflections on loneliness. Likewise, the Bible has many examples of such feelings. King David wrote, "My lovers and my friends stand aloof from my sore; and my kinsmen stand afar off" (Psalm 38:11). "I watch, and am as a sparrow alone upon the house top" (Psalm 102:7). In Psalm 142:4, David uttered what must be the saddest phrase known to mankind: "I looked on my right hand, and beheld, but there was no man that would know me: refuge failed me; no man cared for my soul."

During the Lord's worst moments of separation and loneliness, Matthew records, "Then all the disciples forsook him, and fled" (26:56).

Paul, who had given his post-salvation life to taking the Good News to an entire generation, wrote from a soul-branded loneliness during his final days of life in a Roman prison: "At my first answer no man stood with me, but all men forsook me: I pray God that it may not be laid to their charge" (2 Timothy 4:16).

Knowing that all people experience loneliness in varying degrees, an overcomer must realize that life can be very bleak. There must be a better way.

FRIENDSHIP

"People are lonely," John Newton once wrote, "because they build walls instead of bridges." Or, to put it another way, if we spend many years building those walls around ourselves, our businesses, our futures, our families and our possessions, we have little right to complain when the "things" of life let us down and we're left feeling lonely.

Solomon, the wise king, wrote about that kind of loneliness:

> Two are better than one; because they have a good reward for their labour. For if they fall, the one will lift up his fellow: but woe to him that is alone when he falleth; for he hath not another to help him up (Ecclesiastes 4:9,10).

"The only way to have a friend," Emerson quipped, "is to be one." That's the difficult part. Friendship is a responsibility, not an opportunity. Still, friendship is a treasure ship that anyone can launch no matter what age, race, sex, social standing, religion or success a person might be. Millions of human beings are yearning for a true friend, yet many of those millions are very, very alone.

We all have an innate need to be accepted as a friend. Each of us has the desire and knows the necessity of sharing life's fears, frustrations, victories, hopes and worries. Confession is a form of catharsis. Friendship is the great cure for loneliness. We were created by God for fellowship. No man is an island. We are, like it or not, part of the extended human family. Self-dependence that is expressed as independence from God and His family breeds loneliness.

We can only wonder what would happen if, one-by-one, God's children would take the initiative to befriend at least one other person. The geometric possibilities could revolutionize the world in a brief time.

A SHOULDER TO CRY ON

"But I've really tried to make friends," a reader may

insist. "It's just not that easy to get people to like me." Dale Carnegie had one of the wisest answers to that age-old question of winning friendships: "You can make more friends in two months by becoming interested in other people than you can in two years by trying to get people interested in you." It's such a simple principle, yet so few people seem willing to make the effort to follow it and listen to others.

Isn't it amazing that despite all the speech courses available in education and industry, few schools or companies offer instructional guidelines in the art of listening? It only makes sense that people will seldom be interested in another unless that individual first shows empathy to them. Merely glad-handing and trying to impress others hardly creates interest in us, and that method will definitely not produce any sincere friendships. Rather, a wise person who wants to make friends will capitalize on the natural inclination in others to speak.

Listening to what that potential friend is saying transcends body language, smiling, head-nodding and enthusiasm. Listening is an exciting form of communication and should be practiced often. And the key is, it must be practiced.

Listening works! One has only to ask a few simple questions to get most people involved in a lively conversation. It is true that some won't return the communication, and not every attempt will result in a lasting friendship, but those who take part will go away enriched for having spent time with another who listened.

THE IMPORTANCE OF NAMES

What's in a name? Why are we so interested in names? Is it some inner vacuum that desires recognition?

Who doesn't reach for the new telephone directory and check to make sure his name is there and spelled correctly? Perhaps that same hidden inclination demands that we search a group picture for our own face first.

And yet few people make it a habit to extend the basic courtesy of saying a person's name in conversation. Psychologists report that something special inside us is released whenever we hear someone repeat our name.

Another secret, then, to making friends by being a friend is to make a conscious effort to frequently use the other person's name during conversations. Though it takes a valiant effort to associate or employ memory methods (and there are numerous memory-teaching books available from such authorities as Jerry Lucas and Billy Burden), that simple "secret" can form the basis for hundreds of potential friendships.

In our rush-rush society, a person who takes the extra initiative to remember and use another's name will soon attract friends in much the same way as a lighthouse beacon draws weary ships. And a friendly smile helps, too!

DIVINE FRIEND

"But I've tried all those things," one might say, "and I'm still lonely." Though the circumstances may vary from time to time, the principles do work. Still, the greatest lesson in friendship comes from God. Jesus said these striking words: "Greater love hath no man than this, that a man lay down his life for his friends. Ye are my friends, if ye do whatsoever I command you" (John 15:13,14).

God also promised, "I will never leave thee, nor forsake thee" (Hebrews 13:5). He spoke those words in spite of the age-old rejection that He has received from mankind. Certainly "Amazing Grace" is more than a mere song!

God continues to care, even when we run from Him. His love and friendship seem eternally one-sided, yet He has persisted for centuries. He gave His only begotten Son so that we might accept His pardon and love relationship. He gave His Holy Spirit as our comforter and guide. Through all that, God purposes that we should love Him, not just the things He gives us. He desires our willful love and friendship. God is our example. If He can be so forbearing and forgiving, how can we give up on others because of a few spurned gestures?

We have Him as our friend, and though we may be alone (humanly speaking) at times, we need never be lonely.

TIME

It's natural to want to find and adopt new friends as we go through life's passages. The apostle Paul and Barnabas were very close for several years, but time and circumstances changed things. Each found new interests and pursuits. Paul began working more closely with Silas. Barnabas found Mark.

Although it would be nice to maintain close friendships with the same people throughout life, that seems to be the exception, especially in our transient society. Changes, however, should never become grounds for long-term grief. Someone who moves out of one's life leaves a place for another who needs a friend. At least that's the way it should work. One cannot (indeed, must not) stop developing and risk leaving out friendless people who are in need.

For the Christian, friendliness is not an option. The Christian's life is the world's Bible. Next to the might of

God's Spirit, the silent beauty of a caring, concerned believer is the most powerful influence in the world. A person cannot touch his neighbor's heart with anything less than his own.

How can a person have power to cope with loneliness? He must keep friendship's light shining. God will put it where it will be seen. The only preparation for tomorrow is the proper use of today. God places the emphasis on the *now* of life's day, and on friendships.

POWER PRINCIPLES

I can face my loneliness through a realistic examination of the causes, searching for solutions, not scapegoats.

I can release loneliness through trusting in God's design and forgiveness, and by forgiving those who may have caused (or so I may have thought) me to be alone.

I must rely on God to help me cope with the times when I am alone (or feel alone), always realizing He is more interested in my growth than in my comfort. I know that I can be alone without being lonely.

I can strengthen my healing from loneliness by reaching out to others who are alone and friendless.

A POWER PROMISE

A man that hath friends must shew himself friendly: and there is a friend that sticketh closer than a brother (Proverbs 18:24).

A PRAYER FOR POWER TO COPE
WITH LONELINESS

God, I need Your presence. Forgive me for rejecting You at so many crossroads of my life.

Thank You for caring enough to be with me and for taking away the pain of loneliness.

Most of all, help me bring friendship to others and to be an instrument of Your divine love. Amen.

10

POWER TO COPE WITH TEMPTATION & GUILT

On July 21, 1976, former Georgia Governor and then Presidential candidate Jimmy Carter responded to a question about his beliefs: "I've looked on a lot of women with lust. I've committed adultery in my heart many times. This is something that God recognizes I will do, and I have done it — and God forgives me for it."

That reporter-enticed confession was published in *Playboy* Magazine and quickly made screaming headlines around the world. The public response was puzzling at best.

Christians seemed embarrassed that the candidate from Plains, Georgia, had actually verbalized to the world what we had taught in Sunday school (and what Jesus referred to in Matthew 5:27,28).

Millions of "hip" members of the "me" generation, on the other hand, snickered in disbelief that a national figure could be so out of touch with modern sexual practices, or that Carter would actually feel remorse over thinking about having sex with someone other than his wife, or that there was any need to recognize the guilt at all.

BLIND LEADERS OF THE BLIND

Soon-to-be-President Carter's confession was courageous, especially considering the furor his words created. Perhaps more than anything else, his comments on lust, temptation and guilt brought to focus what could be one of the greatest (and most ignored) problems with which modern man must deal. And one of the aggravating factors with this problem is that there are few leaders willing to take such a courageous stand.

Only 40 percent of college religion teachers and pastoral counselors who responded to a recent survey believed that it is immoral for an unmarried man and woman to have sexual relations. Sidney Buchanan, a University of Houston Law professor, conducted the survey and found some other things that were almost as interesting:

- Nearly half the respondents believed that homosexual relations are not immoral.
- Only about half the teachers and counselors thought the legal system should limit marriage to opposite-sex couples.
- Seventy-one percent replied that they would approve of a known male homosexual teaching elementary school.

"Of those who responded," Buchanan reported, "nearly all were clergy in the sense of having a doctor of divinity degree. Theology was their major area of study." Respondents to the survey represented the broad range of America's denominations including Roman Catholic, Methodist, Baptist and Presbyterian.[1]

THE COST OF "FREEDOM"

Few have bothered to examine realistically the results

of mankind's "new" freedoms. Counselors wink at illicit sex practices and the problems of pornography, then act bewildered as serious sexual crimes involving incest, rape and child molestation reach epidemic stages. Our courts use sterile-sounding terms such as "fetus" and "termination" in legalizing millions of abortions, yet no one knows the mental havoc generated in the lives of countless young women who instinctively know, despite all the legal and professional assurances, that something is wrong with "terminating" that living "organism."

"Freedom" isn't really free. No matter how blasé mankind tries to become about sin, that neatly packaged lifestyle eventually begins coming apart at the seams — for everyone.

Quoting from Mel White's book *Lust: The Other Side of Love:*

> Jimmy Carter's confession made a lot of people laugh. But his words reminded all of us that for four thousand years our Hebrew-Christian tradition has consistently warned us against the results of "doing what comes naturally" without ethical guidelines and restraints. Bible stories tell in lurid detail the horror and heartbreak of runaway sexual lust. The collected wisdom of two thousand years of biblical history from Abraham to Jesus confronts our modern sexual standards and confirms our fears that sexual lust is not a silly outdated notion. Lust is an evil force working to destroy individuals, families, cities, and nations. And the louder we laugh at another man's confession, the more we show our own weakness and vulnerability.[2]

The guilt from such "freedoms" can hardly be relegated to sexual lusts. Many people get so occupied with other "freedoms" that the sexual temptations seem small in comparison: compulsive gamblers, drug addicts, alcoholics, workaholics, even religious or political zealots. The world is full of directions we can take, but people are continually confronted with the lie that there are no rights and wrongs, no goods or bads.

But so many people continue to get hurt from guideline-less "freedoms." The rising statistics on emotional breakdowns, divorces, child abuse, AIDS, suicides and crime all point to the tremendous price we pay for trying to live without restraints.

INSTANT ANSWERS

Perhaps one of the reasons Christians reacted as they did to Carter's confession was that he rebuffed one of the cherished beliefs held by many "born again" believers. Quoting again from Mel White:

> By admitting his own ongoing struggle with lust, he refused to endorse those of his fellow Christians who — in their zeal to oppose the "new morality" — tend to oversimplify the answer by promising, in rebirth or in a second religious experience, an instant, miraculous end to temptation.[3]

Jesus is the "instant answer"; He must deal with human beings, however, and we don't become perfect in a heartbeat. Therein lies the continuing problem of temptation and guilt.

THE LEGAL ASPECT

God's Word declares, and human experience demonstrates, that all men are guilty of sin:

As it is written, There is none righteous, no, not one (Romans 3:10).

For all have sinned, and come short of the glory of God (Romans 3:23).

If we claim to be without sin, we deceive ourselves and the truth is not in us. (1 John 1:8, NIV)

His Word also affirms the clear-cut gospel of redemption from guilt and sin: "If we confess our sins, he is faithful and just and will forgive us our sins and purify us from all unrighteousness" (1 John 1:9, NIV).

Contemporary philosophers look at guilt as something subjective: a feeling, a conditioned response, a result of training. Such thought has been popularized because it removes the burden of blame from the individual. No-fault terminology has even permeated America's judicial system. Former Supreme Court Chief Justice Warren Burger referred to this problem recently in a major speech. He remarked that the judicial system of the United States is totally impotent in dealing with the problem of crime.

The problem with such a system is that *there's no way for things to improve if authorities begin with the presupposition that a person is not ultimately responsible for what he does* — that no matter what he does, his behavior is a result of conditioning and he is therefore not personally guilty. Blame is instead placed on his parents, the environment or society.

With such a presupposition, nobody is totally responsible. In such a society, deterioration and erosion of basic rights and wrongs can only lead to chaos.

However, from the Scripture verses just presented, we see that God holds each individual accountable for his or her deeds. Though we are indeed children of Adam and Eve through whom sin passed upon all mankind, each individual who has ever lived also sins by choice.

So the Good News is not an indictment of man's condition. It is rather a clarification of man's blindness, stubborn will and ignorance. Thankfully, the gospel also presents the answer, the power to deal with temptation and guilt.

FREEDOM FROM GUILT

Guilt is a very painful burden and is also very delusive. Saying goodbye to guilt is especially difficult.

A woman spoke to me after an evening service. "For thirty years I have held something against my sister," she said, "and I want you to know, Pastor, that before I came to the service tonight, I called her. I have wondered why, through all these years, I was constantly bitter and irritable. As you know, I came to the Lord recently, and I then began to realize that I needed to call my sister and tell her I had been holding a grudge against her."

The woman began weeping uncontrollably, and when she finally regained her composure, I asked her what had happened during the telephone conversation.

"She forgave me!" she blurted. "And she even asked me to forgive her! We are getting together to start all over again." The lady looked at me quizzically. "And you know what?" she said.

"What?"

"I held that grudge all those years, and I found out that my sister didn't even know that I was angry at what she had done. Furthermore, she didn't even do what I thought she had done to start with! Can you believe that — thirty years, all gone, because of a misunderstanding?"

The lost years in these sisters' relationship had produced an enormous, elusive barrier of guilt between them. The fact that they were siblings only aggravated the guilt. Thankfully, God broke through the barrier, shattering the guilt.

I remember another lady who found Christ several years ago during a morning church service. Something marvelous happened when she uttered these three words: "God, save me!"

"I had felt such a burden for so many years," the woman told me after the service, "but I didn't know what caused it. Only now do I realize what has been bothering me — I've had several abortions." Suddenly she began crying again.

"Oh, it feels so good to be rid of that guilt," she said eventually. "I had no idea that I had even done anything wrong — it's so socially accepted — but I must have known, deep inside."

I have seen similar experiences with other people who have asked for forgiveness (either from God or man) for all kinds of wrongs — sexual sins, embezzlement, dishonesty, child abuse, gambling, academic cheating; the list goes on and on. To be able to get free of guilt! I've had people describe the burdens of guilt in so many ways. A hangup, a lump in the throat, feeling as if a mountain of weight were on one's back are just a few of them.

In the *Los Angeles Times* one day in April 1967, a front page spread included the tragic photograph of grieving parents who were attending the burial of their son. The accompanying account revealed the sad tale of the young man who had hanged himself out of guilt and frustration after his arrest. The most poignant part of the story was that the youth had killed himself because of a mistaken arrest on a charge that had already been dropped from the books.

How like that young man we all are! We carry excess guilt baggage for things we've done, and sometimes for things we haven't done, when the solution has already been provided. "Therefore being justified by faith, we have peace with God through our Lord Jesus Christ" (Romans 5:1).

Justification — what a magnificent, eternal and exciting word! The apostle Paul, the most educated of the writers in Scripture, used a legal term. A guilty person, according to the full use of the word, isn't just excused, but also pardoned. He doesn't merely "get off the hook," but the guilt is eradicated, expunged, removed completely from any record whatsoever! Bible college students use word association to remember the meaning of justification: "just as if I had never sinned." That definition remains one of the best.

THE PAYMENT FOR GUILT

Years ago, Nicholas I was czar of Russia. Though few of his citizenry knew, it was his habit to strip himself of his royal garments and don the uniform of an army officer from time to time. He would then walk among his soldiers to talk and discover their conditions and morale.

At one point a son of some close friends of the czar was a soldier assigned to a border stockade. There this young man developed several bad habits, one of which was gambling. Though the young man's father was wealthy, the soldier wasted his own portion of the family's money. Further, he embezzled money from the army.

One day, the young soldier received an official notice

that a ranking government authority was on his way to the fortress to examine the army's record books. The young man knew, at that moment, that he would be discovered, dishonored and possibly executed for his dishonesty. In his room that night, he sat down with his books and carefully listed all the money he owed to the army. With a heavy heart, he finally wrote these words under the total: "A great debt! Who can pay it?"

He sat for hours looking at the ledger and the note, obviously filled with despair at what would happen the next day when the official arrived. Finally, overpowered with the ponderous cares, he fell asleep.

That particular night, Czar Nicholas, on one of his occasional incognito inspections, entered the border stockade and noticed the light still burning in one of the offices. He entered the room and noticed his friend's son asleep at the table, his head buried in his arms. Then he spied the paper with the figures and the painfully written note.

Reading those words and seeing the exhausted young man, the czar was moved with pity. Quickly, he picked up the pen and wrote one word directly underneath the question: "Nicholas!"

Soon the young soldier awakened. Reaching for his pistol, he fully intended to take his own life rather than face certain dishonor and public punishment. Then his eyes looked again at the paper and noticed the czar's signature. "Can it be true?" he uttered. And at that moment he knew the czar must have been there during the night.

"Then he knows all about the debt," the young man continued to himself, "and yet he is willing to pay it all!" It seemed too good to be true. Within a short time, however, a messenger from the czar arrived at the border fortress. He delivered a sack of gold to the soldier, and in the bag was an amount exactly equal to the debt figure he had written the night before.

In a similar but much greater way, Jesus died to pay the certain penalty for our sins. He was the propitiation (another legal term Paul used in his letter to the Romans), or substitute, who satisfied God's wrath against our sins.

John Wesley wrote, "In my place condemned He stood. Hallelujah! What a Savior!" But a gift is not truly a gift until it is received.

CONFESSION

"Okay," you may say, "I can confess to God, asking for His free gift of salvation, knowing that He has provided His Son as my payment for sin. I can be rid of guilt. But what about that daily struggle with temptation? When I give in, guilt comes again. It's a vicious cycle."

Christians, those who are honest, realize just how vicious that struggle can be. So we live in isolation, members of the church, all dressed up, all respectable. At the same time, we all go through the continual progression of human temptations.

Just as there's an answer to the problem of sin (salvation), there's also a solution to the ongoing struggle with daily temptations and the guilt that results when we fail. "If we confess our sins, He is faithful and just to forgive us our sins, and to cleanse us from all unrighteousness" (1 John 1:9). The confession must be an ongoing, daily practice. Without continual cleansing, the Christian becomes a stagnant, smelly pond.

But there's more.

Confess to one another therefore your faults —

your slips, your false steps, your offenses, your sins;
and pray [also] for one another, that you may be
healed *and* restored — to a spiritual tone of mind
and heart (James 5:16a, AMP).

Until a person finds a portion of the Christian community
with whom he can talk freely (his wife, a pastor or
counselor, or a "cell" group), he will never discover the
true meaning of overcoming temptation and guilt.

Certainly, we cannot confess to just anyone. There
are gossips within the church, just like anywhere else.
The details of one's struggles are not the business of
everyone; still, we don't have to be alone with our secret
struggles. Starting with a trusted Christian counselor can
be the beginning, but there are many untrained brothers
and sisters in Christ who are specially gifted for listening.
Knowing there's even just one other person who's familiar
with our struggles, who's praying for us and whom we're
accountable to on a regular basis provides a tremendous
motivation for saying no to temptation. There is strength
in numbers.

POWER PRINCIPLES

I can face guilt and temptation through a realistic
examination of my faults and needs (especially my sinful
human nature), realizing that God is interested in me as
an individual.

I can release temptation and guilt through trusting
in God's forgiveness, and by forgiving those who may
have been partially responsible for my struggles (though
I must always be aware that I have a choice each time
when it comes to sin).

I must rely on God to help me cope with my temptations and guilts, always realizing He is more interested in my growth than in my comfort.

I can strengthen my healing from temptation and guilt by reaching out to others in the midst of their struggles, burdens and lusts.

POWER PROMISES

Be kind and compassionate to one another, forgiving each other, just as in Christ God forgave you (Ephesians 4:32, NIV).

Therefore [there is] now no condemnation — no adjudging guilty of wrong — for those who are in Christ Jesus, *who live not after the dictates of the flesh, but after the dictates of the Spirit* (Romans 8:1, AMP).

A PRAYER FOR POWER TO COPE WITH TEMPTATION AND GUILT

Father, receive my thanks for justifying me, for redeeming me, for buying my freedom and for cancelling my guilt-ridden debt.

Lord, help me not to hold grudges against others. Help me not to make others feel guilty by judging them. Help me to free others when they have failed. Immerse me today in love and forgiveness and grace.

Most of all, help me to cope with my temptation and guilt, and give me strength to forgive others as You have forgiven me. Amen.

11

POWER TO COPE
WITH DEATH & LOSS

"**T**o every thing there is a season, and a time
to every purpose under the heaven. A time to be born,
and a time to die" (Ecclesiastes 3:1,2a).

When I remember all
The friends, so link'd together,
I've seen around me fall,
Like leaves in wintry weather,
I feel like one
Who treads alone
Some banquet-hall deserted
— Morre,
"Oft in the Stilly Night"

I have a rendezvous with Death
At some disputed barricade . . .
And I to my pledged word am true,
I shall not fail that rendezvous.
— Alan Seeger,
"I Have a Rendezvous
with Death"

The prospect of death is not something to which people look forward. Some feel that next to dying, the awareness of getting older is the greatest shock one can experience. The cosmetic industry, now grossing over $6 billion a year, is largely aimed at that awareness.

Life, according to the Bible, is a shadow (1 Chronicles 29:15), like a weaver's flying shuttle (Job 7:6), like hurrying messengers (Job 9:25) and like a vanishing vapor: "Whereas ye know not what shall be on the morrow. For what is your life? It is even a vapor, that appeareth for a little time, and then vanisheth away" (James 4:14).

When a Christian dies, death is not a tragedy. It is a victory, a leaving for a better home (Hebrews 11:16). Jesus' crucifixion on the cross and His subsequent resurrection destroyed the sting of death for His followers. Death, since then, is not the end of life; it is the beginning of eternal life in heaven with Him. "For God so loved the world that he gave his one and only Son, that whoever believes in him shall not perish but have eternal life" (John 3:16, NIV).

Throughout the New Testament, believers who had to face death were ready, yielding and eager to meet the Savior. Perhaps the most outstanding example of this is the account of Stephen's death as recorded in the book of Acts:

> But he [Stephen], full of the Holy Spirit and controlled by [Him], gazed into heaven and saw the glory — the splendor and majesty — of God, and Jesus standing at God's right hand; And he said, Look! I see the heavens opened, and the Son of man standing at God's right hand! . . . And while they were stoning Stephen, he prayed, Lord Jesus, receive *and* accept *and* welcome my spirit! And

falling on his knees, he cried out loudly, Lord, fix
not this sin upon them — lay it not to their charge!
And when he had said this, he fell asleep [in death]
(Acts 7:55,56,59,60, AMP).

As Paul the apostle faced certain death at the hands
of his Roman captors, he issued an unusual statement:

For I am now ready to be offered, and the time
of my departure is at hand. I have fought a good
fight, I have finished my course, I have kept the
faith: Henceforth there is laid up for me a crown
of righteousness, which the Lord, the righteous
judge, shall give me at that day: and not to me
only, but unto all them also that love his appearing
(2 Timothy 4:6-8).

"I see the heavens opened!" "I am now ready!" If
only we could face death with that much confidence! Is
it possible? A careful search through the Bible reveals
many assurances for the believer.

A TIME TO DIE

Coping with anything, we have learned, must begin
with a realistic understanding of that subject. The most
realistic, sobering part of life is that death is inevitable.
"It is appointed unto men once to die" (Hebrews 9:27).
Death, we're told, came upon mankind because of Adam's
willful sin: "Wherefore, as by one man sin entered into
the world, and death by sin; and so death passed upon
all men, for that all have sinned" (Romans 5:12).

The gloomy death sentence, however, has been replaced by God's promise of life — all because Jesus paid
the penalty for sin and death on Calvary's cross:

Take notice! I tell you a mystery — a secret truth, an event decreed by the hidden purpose or counsel of God. We shall not all fall asleep [in death], but we shall all be changed (transformed) . . . O death, where is your victory? O death, where is your sting? Now sin is the sting of death, and sin exercises its power [upon the soul] through [the abuse of] the Law. But thanks be to God, Who gives us the victory — making us conquerors — through our Lord Jesus Christ (1 Corinthians 15:51, 55-57, AMP).

How exciting to know that our earthly bodies will be replaced by heavenly bodies that will never die, and that we shall be forevermore in the presence of the Lord! Small wonder that David wrote, "Precious in the sight of the LORD is the death of his saints" (Psalm 116:15). "For me to live is Christ," Paul wrote, "and to die is gain" (Philippians 1:21).

Just as God offers life everlasting, however, He also allows man to make a choice. The wrong decision has but one horrible result:

> Whoever believes and is baptized will be saved, but whoever does not believe will be condemned (Mark 16:16, NIV).
> Whoever believes in him is not condemned, but whoever does not believe stands condemned already because he has not believed in the name of God's one and only Son (John 3:18, NIV).
> And death and hell were cast into the lake of fire. This is the second death. And whosoever was not found written in the book of life was cast into the lake of fire (Revelation 20: 14,15).

With such a clear-cut choice, there's certainly no rational reason for refusing to accept God's simple solution to the problem of inevitable death.

> I assure you, most solemnly I tell you, the person whose ears are open to My words — who listens to My message — and believes *and* trusts in *and* clings to *and* relies on Him Who sent Me has (possesses now) eternal life. And he does not come into judgment — does not incur sentence of judgment, will not come under condemnation — but he has already passed over out of death into life (John 5:24, AMP).

GRIEF

But what about those who are left to face the death of that loved one? Grief is a traumatic experience and can often consume a person.

One of the self-acknowledged purposes for Jesus' coming to earth, according to a prophecy in Isaiah 61:2, was to "comfort all that mourn." The second of His Beatitudes expressed the sympathy and compassion Jesus felt: "Blessed are they that mourn: for they shall be comforted" (Matthew 5:4). At the grave of Lazarus Jesus wept (John 11:35). Jesus knew the depths of grief. When He died on the cross, the "Man of Sorrows" actually bore all of our griefs and sorrows. Why? That we might be healed (Isaiah 53).

There is a natural period of grief, of course, when a family member or friend passes away, but the healing process also begins immediately. "Weeping may endure for a night," the psalmist assured, "but joy cometh in the morning" (Psalm 30:5). The grief will not, must not, cannot last forever. No matter how difficult or painful the loss of a loved one may be, life goes on. The pain eventually subsides. In perspective, especially when the death involves a Christian, joy will come as we dwell on the wonderful, eternal life that loved one is now embracing.

We can be thankful that God has promised to bring a supernatural comfort as we endure the sorrow. He is, according to 2 Corinthians 1:3, the "God of all comfort."

Furthermore, God will bring that comfort to His children so that we can help others as we identify with their suffering:

> [God] Who consoles *and* comforts *and* encourages us in every trouble (calamity and affliction), so that we may also be able to console (comfort and encourage) those who are in any kind of trouble or distress, with the consolation (comfort and encouragement) with which we ourselves are consoled *and* comforted *and* encouraged by God (2 Corinthians 1:4, AMP).

Life does go on, no matter how painful the moments of grief might be. The overcomer needs to face the reality of death, and endure the struggle with grief. Gratefully, we can look forward in faith to a time when death, grief, hurts, and sorrow will be forgotten: "He will wipe every tear from their eyes. There will be no more death or mourning or crying or pain, for the old order of things has passed away" (Revelation 21:4, NIV).

POWER PRINCIPLES

I can face death and grief through a realistic examination of the inevitability of death, remembering that life does go on.

I can release my fear of death and the struggle with grief through trusting in God's forgiveness and His healing power, and by forgiving those who may have contributed to the pain that I feel, remembering that it is relatively common for people to harbor secret resentments against either God or the loved one who passed away.

I must rely on God to help me cope with these areas, always realizing He is more interested in my growth than in my comfort.

I can strengthen the healing of grief by reaching out and understanding others in the midst of their pain.

A POWER PROMISE

He that overcometh shall inherit all things;
and I will be his God, and he shall be my son.
(Revelation 21:7).

A PRAYER FOR POWER TO COPE
WITH DEATH AND GRIEF

Lord, You are the Creator of the mystery of life. I realize that I cannot control life or death; therefore, I must look to You for strength to live life to the fullest, and I can cling to Your blessed promise of everlasting life after death.

When I grieve for departed loved ones, give me the assurance that the pain will lessen as I continue to turn to You.

And help me grasp the needs of those grieving people around me, especially those who do not know You and who do not have the blessed hope for eternity. Help me to share Your plan of redemption with them. Amen.

12

POWER TO COPE WITH UNFORGIVENESS

During my early life, I was detached from my family and adrift emotionally. My two sisters were ten and twelve years older than me, and a third sister had died as a child. Since I was rather late in coming, and since my father had a busy law practice, I had trouble relating to my family.

As a young teenager, I got mixed up in the wrong kind of activities, and along with two other teenagers, I was arrested once. I was an eighth grader at the time.

Because my father was a well-known lawyer, and since he knew the judge, I was allowed to go to military school instead of a reform school. It was there that I spent my high school years. By the time I was sixteen, I began to work and pay my own way through the military institution.

It was also during this time that I accepted Jesus Christ. I'm thankful that as He and I teamed together to turn my life around, many good things began happening. I was given the school's highest honors, graduated as class captain and offered an appointment to the U.S. Military Academy at West Point.

But God had other plans for me. My grandmother had heard of Wheaton College and wanted me to go there.

Since I was also beginning to feel the compulsion to enter the ministry, I transferred to that Bible school. It was there that God taught me many great lessons, often through the worst struggles.

For some reason, "Nuts" McGrab, a great soccer player, and I rubbed each other the wrong way from the beginning. Quite simply, I got on his nerves and vice versa. We didn't come to blows, but the edginess was constant.

Then, on a Sunday morning during that first year at Wheaton, I received a telephone call with the news that my mother had fallen in a snowstorm and died from the resulting injuries. I was devastated and hurried home to Pennsylvania for the funeral.

When I returned to college, I discovered that "Nuts" had also lost his mother that same week. When we both came back to the campus, broken and shattered as any college students would be when something that inexplicable and unexpected takes place, he and I were seized by the common spasm of sorrow. We were driven to forgiveness of each other. Immediately we became loving Christian brothers (as we should have been before).

Through that simple act of forgiveness, an entire chain of events transpired. I began seeing myself in a different light. I started discovering just how many burdens of unforgiveness I had carried around for so many years.

A little poem I wrote then ably expressed how I felt (and still feel):

> It was a joy in life to find
> That on the journey of the road,
> The strong arms of comrades bind
> To help me onward with my load.

And since I have no gold to give,
And love alone must make amends,
I ask of God that while I live
He make me grateful for my friends.

Thank God, I learned early in life that forgiveness is more than the remission of anger and injustice. It should also mean the restoration of a broken fellowship.

Therefore, as God's chosen people, holy and dearly loved, clothe yourselves with compassion, kindness, humility, gentleness and patience. Bear with each other and forgive whatever grievances you may have against one another. Forgive as the Lord forgave you. And over all these virtues put on love, which binds them all together in perfect unity (Colossians 3:12-14, NIV).

PATTERN OF FORGIVENESS

"Forgiveness is man's deepest need," Horace Bushnell once wrote, "and highest achievement." Forgiveness brings a release of one's debt. It's mentioned little in the Old Testament, though the story of Joseph points to that virtue. As a result of his brothers' building resentment, Joseph was sold to some caravan traders who took him down to Egypt. There he was unjustly accused of a crime and sent to prison. For years he was forgotten. Times changed, however, and after he was placed in a position of power, a famine struck the Mideast and Joseph's brothers had to go down to Egypt. There, after a painful process, Joseph forgave his brothers during a tearful reunion.

All forgiveness is premised on the fact that the person who must be forgiven is often undeserving and even unwilling to recognize he needs to be forgiven.

That's what is so incorrigible about modern man. Human nature assumes that God (or another person) is always in the wrong — that God (or the other person) should always take the first step in any forgiveness.

In Matthew 18, the writer recorded a story Jesus once told about a very wealthy man, a ruler who was called "lord," who was owed $15 million by a servant. "I can't pay it," the servant said when it came time to pay off the debt.

"That's all right," replied the ruler. "I will forgive you."

Then, according to the parable told by Jesus, that same servant turned around to a fellow servant. "You owe me twenty-five dollars," said the servant whose own debt had just been forgiven. "Pay up or else."

"Wait," pleaded the fellow servant, "I just don't have any money. Can you give me a little more time?"

"No!" he said. The first servant then had his co-worker put in prison.

Well, the ruler was furious when he heard the details, so he called his servant in and told him, "I'm going to make you pay."

The contrast between $15 million and $25 was staggering, and Jesus told the story that way to make the illustration absolutely clear. Then the Savior said, "So likewise shall my heavenly Father do also unto you, if ye from your hearts forgive not every one his brother their trespasses" (Matthew 18:35).

When we fail to forgive somebody, it's often due to a psychological effort to manipulate and control that person. There's a sense in which our lack of forgiveness pushes the other person into a hostage position. We put him below us. We want to keep an I. O. U. hanging over that person's head in judgment. We desire to be strong, to have one step up.

Jesus knew the manipulative drive within each of us. That was why He told the parable. He wanted us to realize that unforgiveness is an evil, divisive experience. Only as we see the dark side can we understand how gloriously grand are the gifts of forgiveness that God has for us and that we need to give to each other.

FORGIVENESS FRACTURED

What keeps forgiveness from being offered? Why doesn't it flow freely? A careful examination of Jesus' parable reflects the problems that can hinder forgiveness.

First, too often we fail to forgive when we focus on the problem, not the person. Instead of seeing his fellow servant through eyes of compassion as his ruler had, the just-forgiven servant concentrated on the twenty-five dollars owed to him. The law of reciprocity suggests that as forgiveness was extended to him, he should have passed it on to his co-worker. Fractured forgiveness doesn't do that. It focuses on the problem.

Second, an unforgiving person overlooks his own responsibility and always blames the other person. Jesus spoke of the speck versus the two-by-four, the little spot in the eye versus the huge beam. It's always easy to do that. We tend to ignore our own weaknesses while maximizing the problems of others.

Third, since we want to believe that the problem is always with the other person, we wait for him to ask, speak and mediate. We want him to take the first step forward, thereby lessening the chance of our getting hurt. Thank God that He didn't wait for us to apologize before offering forgiveness! And He's our model.

Fourth, an unforgiving person thinks he has the

right to judge. When we fail to forgive someone, we're assuming that we know all the facts, that it's obvious where the fault lies — a dubious assumption, to say the least.

Fifth, one must notice from Jesus' story that what a person sows, he reaps. When we sow resentment and resistance instead of forgiveness, it almost always boomerangs on us.

REMISSION

Jesus' manner was forgiveness. That was what He taught and practiced. When the woman was taken in adultery, He said, "Neither do I condemn thee" (John 8:11). Zaccheus, the head of the Jerusalem syndicate, sought Him, and the Savior urged, "Come down from the tree — I will have dinner with you" (see Luke 19:5). Even when Peter denied Him, the risen Christ appeared to the disciple with forgiveness freely offered.

Jesus' ministry was forgiveness. "Give us this day our daily bread. And forgive us our debts as we forgive our debtors," He taught us to pray (Matthew 6:11,12). "Thy sins be forgiven thee . . . who can forgive sins but God only?" (Mark 2:5,7). The last words of Jesus before ascending — the command to preach repentance and remission of sins in His name — were filled with forgiveness.

Remission is the Hebrew and Greek concept of dispatching — putting a letter in the mail box to send it away. God offers the incredible miracle of remission for our sins, promising that our sins can be buried in the deepest sea, covered with a thick cloud, blotted out, expunged and washed whiter than snow. "As far as the east is from the west," the psalmist assured, "so far hath he removed our transgressions from us" (Psalm 103:12).

FORGIVING OTHERS

As Christ acted toward us, so He has called His children to act. Forgiveness, for the Christian, should be as natural, beautiful and normal as are breathing, eating and sleeping. In practical terms, God (through the pen of Paul) explained His standard for us: "Be ye kind one to another, tenderhearted, forgiving one another, even as God for Christ's sake hath forgiven you" (Ephesians 4:32).

All Christians, especially those who desire a deeper walk with the Lord, know what it's like to be forgiven a huge debt that could never be repaid. However, some of us are still holding petty grudges over the heads of fellow human beings. Why do we think that we can be unforgiving toward others and still receive God's full pardon and power?

There are two kinds of Christians, some who have only accepted Jesus Christ as Savior and others who are also seeking to make Him Lord. For Christ to be Lord of a Christian's life, however, the believer must come under the control of the Holy Spirit. May God help us receive His power to cope with resentment and grudges. Only He can resolve our unforgiving attitudes.

> Doing an injury puts you below your enemy;
> Revenging one makes you but even with him;
> Forgiving it sets you above him.
> — Benjamin Franklin

POWER PRINCIPLES

I can cope with unforgiveness through an honest evaluation of the causes, searching for solutions, not scapegoats.

I can release the unforgiveness by first understanding God's amazing act of removing my own debts, then by forgiving those who have wronged me.

I must rely on God to help me cope with the times when it's hardest to forgive (or ask forgiveness), always realizing He is more interested in my growth than in my comfort.

I can strengthen my healing of unforgiveness by reaching out to others caught in the midst of their own hurts.

A POWER PROMISE

Finally, be ye all of one mind, having compassion one of another, love as brethren, be pitiful, be courteous: not rendering evil for evil, or railing for railing: but contrariwise blessing; knowing that ye are thereunto called, that ye should inherit a blessing (1 Peter 3:8,9).

A PRAYER FOR POWER TO COPE
WITH UNFORGIVENESS

May the words of my mouth and the meditation of my heart be acceptable in Your sight, O Lord, My strength and redeemer.

Help me to forgive, even as You have forgiven me, so that the impact of Your forgiveness might be extended to those around me.

May I not only be a hearer of the Word, but a doer also.

As the days become shorter before Your return, help me redeem the time by being a forgiving follower of You. Amen.

13

POWER TO COPE WITH UNREST & WORLD CONDITIONS

The apostle Paul, under the leadership of the Holy Spirit, sat down nearly two thousand years ago and began writing these unsettling words:

> This know also, that in the last days perilous times shall come. For men shall be lovers of their own selves, covetous, boasters, proud, blasphemers, disobedient to parents, unthankful, unholy, without natural affection, trucebreakers, false accusers, incontinent, fierce, despisers of those that are good, traitors, heady, highminded, lovers of pleasures more than lovers of God, having a form of godliness, but denying the power thereof: from such turn away (2 Timothy 3:1-5).

The twentieth century has brought many exciting, beneficial and wonderful advancements. Numerous diseases have been virtually eradicated from entire countries. Electricity, automobiles, trains and airplanes have come into widespread use. The reader of a current newspaper would be at a great disadvantage if he didn't understand such recent vocabulary additions as microchip, laser, fiberoptic, computer and orthoscope. Most Americans get up in the morning with a warm shelter over them; they have many options from which to choose to eat; they often are afforded several different types of transportation. Schools are provided for their children. Most Americans arrive back home in plenty of time to enjoy various recreational outlets — electronic games, television, family activities. Few, very few, go to bed hungry.

But we live in a precarious environment at best. Two thousand years ago, when Paul wrote his second letter to Timothy, the earth contained 300 million people. It took 1700 years to double that figure. By 1820 the world's population exceeded one billion. By 1930, it had doubled again. During the early 1960s three billion people lived on the globe. That number reached four billion during the late '70s. By 1990, the population will exceed five billion, and by the year 2000, it will soar above the six billion figure.

The question, of course, must be this: How can this many people survive? How long can we provide ourselves with enough energy, air, clean water and food to keep everyone alive? We're already seeing the horrible ravages of famine in certain parts of the world; how can we satisfy the hunger of additional billions? Waste disposal and pollution are already critical situations in many urban areas around the world. We can only imagine what mankind will be facing within a few years as the population continues to increase dramatically.

PESSIMISM OR OPTIMISM

How can the Christian cope with unsettling world conditions? And what about atomic technology and "star wars" strategies? How can we face the future with any degree of optimism?

We know Christ assured us that our citizenship is in heaven (Philippians 3:20), but we're currently bound to this earth. What if the world struggles under the multiple curses of pollution, disease, famine and unrest? Does that mean that we simply give up and go live in a survivalist camp somewhere?

Certainly not! The fact that we're citizens of heaven does not negate the fact that we're currently inhabitors of the earth. The promise of heaven doesn't exempt us from daily responsibilities here and now. Quite to the contrary, God desires that we apply scriptural principles to present situations.

> Therefore being justified by faith, we have peace with God through our Lord Jesus Christ: by whom also we have access by faith into this grace wherein we stand, and rejoice in hope of the glory of God. And not only so, but we glory in tribulations also: knowing that tribulation worketh patience; and patience, experience; and experience, hope: and hope maketh not ashamed; because the love of God is shed abroad in our hearts by the Holy Ghost which is given unto us (Romans 5:1-5).

Peace, hope, and love! Therein is the antidote for unrest.

PEACE

If there's a one-word synonym for the Lord Jesus Christ, it's peace. He is called "our peace." That word entails a person, not just a philosophy or principle for life. He's also called "the Prince of Peace." Throughout the Scriptures, we're encouraged to have peace.

The Bible offers many explanations and examples of the use of the word *peace*. When Joshua was going to build an altar (back then an altar was an instant cathedral, a place to worship and pray or a place of memory), he gathered some uncut stones. The Hebrew word *shalom* was used, meaning that the altar was naturally formed, whole, unquarried, not split — a cohesive, natural formation made by God. Peace!

The second time the thought is conveyed in the Bible is in the book of Ruth: "The LORD recompense thy work, and a full reward be given thee of the LORD GOD of Israel, under whose wings thou art come to trust" (Ruth 2:12). The thought given is that God would give a full reward, full payment and totally adequate recognition. Peace!

Nehemiah, the tremendous strategist, went to Jerusalem with the permission of the king of Persia. In fifty-four days he rebuilt the walls of the city with borrowed materials. All during this time, Ezra read the Torah, and the greatest revival that Israel ever experienced took place. Nehemiah wept over the ruins, then built the wall. When the work was completed, he looked at the wall and pronounced, "The wall is shalom. The wall is finished!"

In such contexts, the word *shalom* speaks of wholeness, of a perfectness, of an entirety that is adequate for all our needs. God says that the wholeness He wants to bring to us should be evident in our lives.

In Ephesians 2:14, Paul wrote, "He is our peace . . . and hath broken down the middle wall of partition between us." As such, Jesus Christ has thrown Himself against a barrier that keeps people apart. So when we desire to know Jesus Christ, there must come a oneness, a feeling of wholeness. We ought not to be dealing with the guilt of sin anymore. "If we confess our sins, he is faithful and just to forgive us our sins, and to cleanse us from all unrighteousness" (1 John 1:9). All sins — past, present, and future — are already provided for by Jesus Christ. As Christians, we don't have to spend our lives playing "catch up"; God has already provided for us. We have other, more important things to do.

In the New Testament, we are told twenty-three times that we have the personal responsibility to minister to each other and sustain the peace of God because we are one. God made us to be undivided, to be wholesome, fully-rewarded people, and we should be together within the Christian community. We must see one another as individuals who each play an important role in the complete Body of Christ. There is strength in numbers, but only when Christians unite in love.

HOPE

The second word to be noticed in Romans 5 is "hope." The ground, the very basis for hope, is in the resurrection of Jesus Christ. "Blessed be the God and Father of our Lord Jesus Christ, which according to his abundant mercy hath begotten us again unto a lively hope by the resurrection of Jesus Christ from the dead" (1 Peter 1:3). Hope isn't just a theological term or pious statement; it's an experience. "Christ in you," Paul wrote, "the hope of glory" (Colossians 1:27).

The primary reason the first-century Jews wouldn't accept the preaching of the gospel after Pentecost was that Christians were daring to say that the God of Abraham, Isaac and Jacob had given a Son, a Messiah, who was God incarnate and who died on a cross and rose again.

The Christians undoubtedly began to say, "Do you remember the God who used to live in the temple, whom you had never seen, whose name was above every name, who roared on the mountain and placed a pillar of fire, who divided the seas and dropped heavenly bread like dew on the grass early in the morning and who was like a mighty conqueror for Israel? That God came to earth in the form of a baby, Jesus Christ!"

No wonder it was so difficult for the Jews to accept a Messiah who came from Nazareth — that filthy place. Where were the birth arrangements and announcements? Where did this boy come from? Some said he was the natural son of Joseph. Everything about Him was suspect. How did He dare speak in the temple? He had no credentials. Why should the people there have listened to Him? What school did He graduate from?

But when Jesus lived, moved and operated powerfully as God in the flesh, it was obvious to the crowds that His background wasn't relevant. "Truly," the centurion uttered at Calvary, "this was the Son of God" (Matthew 27:54).

That same God incarnate, Jesus Christ, rose from the grave, ascended into heaven and lives within each of us who have accepted Him as Savior. The ground of hope for us lies in the resurrection of Jesus Christ and the fact that He resides within us.

Our goal of hope is this: We are to be "looking for that blessed hope, and the glorious appearing of the great God and our Saviour Jesus Christ" (Titus 2:13).

What does such a hope do? It purifies us. We learn to be accountable to God, to "redeem the time" (see Ephesians 5:16), as Paul insisted — to buy up every opportunity.

Referring to Romans 5 once more, such a hope "maketh not ashamed." Such hope does not leave the believer in Christ insecure.

LOVE

The third term in Romans 5 that I want to stress is the word "love." "The love of God is shed abroad in our hearts" (Romans 5:5), Paul taught. The words "shed abroad" mean "to pour out."

When Jesus went into the temple and threw over the tables, the money fell on the temple floor. The same word was used there but translated in this context as dumped over, poured, lavishly exposed.

Why would Paul use the same terminology concerning an antidote to unrest? We must understand the word picture: the love of Christ is pouring itself into our lives. What, then, does love do? Our theology becomes wholistic (not holistic!). We have it "together." We can cope because the peace of God is settled down and filling in all the cracks and cavities in our lives. We can have a feeling of being perfected (though not perfect yet) and thoroughly equipped for life because of this harmonious relationship with God. We relate interpersonally with each other — God and us! The living presence of Jesus Christ is in our lives. The coming of the Savior is an anchor that draws us every day into the dock of God.

Here is the love of God, pouring itself out, and what does it do? It gives! Jesus said, "As my Father hath sent me, even so send I you" (John 20:21). The key to a successful Christian experience hinges on a deep, personal relationship with Jesus Christ.

We aren't Christians by coercion. We're Christians by choice. We follow Him because of love. And that love will bring us into tremendous, understanding relationships with others.

Why did Jesus Christ come? He came because of the love of God. And because of His coming, it's possible for each of us to know His love. "Love Me," He insists, "and if you love Me, you will do what I say" (see John 14:15).

Love!

HEART OF GOD

Peace, hope and love. In spite of looming world conditions, the Christian has a supernatural source of all three.

Most of all, however, the Christian has an opportunity to provide a clear witness of Jesus Christ's saving grace. Millions, even billions, of the earth's inhabitants have never heard the gospel, and the Christian has the one lasting answer to unrest, problems and pain. A believer can provide companionship to the lonely, but mainly he can point them to the Lord Jesus, the friend who never fails or forsakes. To the discouraged, the child of God can proclaim the good news that Jesus offers deliverance from the guilt and grip of sin.

It's difficult to stay troubled when busy, and that's also part of God's plan for coping with today's struggles. There is much to be done, especially by the Christian if he's to be an obedient follower of Christ.

"My interest is in the future," Charles Kettering said, "because I am going to spend the rest of my life there!" That's true, but the Bible says "the kingdom of Heaven is at hand," so the Christian begins living and working in the kingdom starting right now, right here on earth.

POWER PRINCIPLES

I can cope with unrest and world conditions through a realistic evaluation of the situation, searching for solutions, not panaceas.

I can release my unrest by first understanding God's design — His forgiveness, His peace, His hope and His love!

I need to rely on God to help me cope with difficult days ahead, always realizing He is more interested in my growth than in my comfort.

I can strengthen my healing of worry over world conditions by reaching out to a world (and my next-door neighbor) caught in the midst of troubling unrest, and by ministering to those who do not know the Savior.

A POWER PROMISE

Looking for that blessed hope, and the glorious appearing of the great God and our Saviour Jesus Christ, who gave himself for us, that he might redeem us from all iniquity, and purify unto himself a peculiar people, zealous of good works (Titus 2:13,14).

A PRAYER FOR POWER TO COPE WITH UNREST AND WORLD CONDITIONS

Heavenly Father, thank You for letting me be one with my brothers and sisters in Christ. There is power and strength in numbers, in being part of the Body of Christ.

Teach me to be peaceful, hopeful and loving. Only then can I become a useful part of the reconciling process in this world.

Use me, I pray, to help mend broken relationships, to strengthen feeble hearts, to share Your peace.

Take Your glorious gifts of peace, hope and love, and baptize me in the reality of what You are, Whom to know is eternal and abundant life. Amen.

14

POWER TO COPE
WITH LIFE

Why do people have to face problems? Why should Christians have to suffer just like anyone else? In his book *The Jesus Generation*, Dr. Billy Graham touched on this key area:

> Jesus didn't use subtlety or gimmicks to gain followers. Rather, He honestly laid before them the tough demands of discipleship — total commitment and total involvement.
>
> Christ lays down conditions, but only a few meet them. Only a few are willing to pay the price. Christ's way is a way of discipline, renunciation, and hardship. The verbs used in the New Testament to describe the Christian life are "fight," "wrestle," "run," "work," "suffer," "endure," "resist," "agonize," "mortify." The Scriptures describe a Christian as a soldier who must suffer hardship. Paul wrote to Timothy: "Thou therefore endure hardness, as a good soldier of Jesus Christ" (2 Timothy 2:3).[1]

Difficulties seem to come in nearly every area of life, usually in direct proportion to the success we hope to attain. For example, if a young man decides he wants to become a football player, he knows that he will face many bumps, bruises and blows. "It's just a part of the game," he explains to his not-so-enthusiastic mother.

Then, if the young man experiences some success in high school and has the opportunity to play college ball, he begins building himself up, pushing himself harder, taking great pains (literally) to achieve his next goal. Less than 2000 young men per year participate in professional football, and those who reach that level are not only the most talented, but also those who have pushed themselves to their physical and emotional limits. There are no "free lunches," especially when it comes to that game, for those who want to succeed.

Or consider the high school girl who decides to become an actress. It's one thing for her friends and family to encourage her with words like "Mary, you've got what it takes to make it all the way to the top. You're a natural." But those loved ones will probably not be there during the thousands of lonely hours of practice, auditions, rejections, weekends with minus-ten dollars in the bank, false hopes, dashed dreams and "Why-don't-you-just-come-home-and-forget-all-that" urgings. The starry-eyed, would-be actress, if realistic, must accept the struggles if she expects stardom. There are no overnight successes.

The professional businessperson who determines to reach the top of the corporate ladder likewise knows that the greater the level of corporate success, the more difficult the climb. The jogger who is inspired to compete in a marathon fully expects to endure sore feet, shin splints, aching muscles, lonely morning runs with dogs snapping at one's sneakers and "Why-would-a-person-your-age-ever-think-of-running-in-a-marathon" stares from friends and family. "No pain, no gain," the runner chants as he pushes himself to each new level of endurance.

The young woman who determines to be the best mother she can be chooses to invest quality time into raising her baby. She realizes that there will be nights spent holding and praying over a sick infant. She understands that it will take much energy to correctly rear that growing child, even though others may not comprehend why she pours her life into such a thankless and misunderstood job. Delayed gratification takes on an entirely new meaning. "But I'm willing to do all that," she insists. "I want to be the best mother I can be."

Life itself is not easy. Success in any area doesn't come without difficulties. Why then do people, once they accept Jesus Christ as Savior, keep asking "Why do I have to go through these struggles? Why does everyone else have it so easy when I have so many battles to face? Why do I have to suffer? After all, I'm a Christian now"?

REASONS

The Bible gives Christians many reasons for why we struggle and suffer:
- to return us to God (Jeremiah 3:22, Hosea 6:1);
- to cause us to pray (Isaiah 26:16);
- to make us compassionate (Hebrews 13:3);
- to bring greater strength (Romans 8:37; Hebrews 12:12,13);
- to glorify God (Psalm 50:15);
- to receive God's glory (2 Corinthians 4:17);
- to be worthy of honor (2 Timothy 2:20,21);
- to make us less offensive (Job 34:31);

- to partake of God's holiness (Hebrews 12:10);
- to pay our vows to God (Psalm 66:11-14);
- to have the power of Christ (2 Corinthians 12:9);
- to receive good (Romans 8:28);
- to repent of sin (Revelation 3:19);
- to reign with Christ (2 Timothy 2:12);
- to be brought to our senses (Luke 15:13-20);
- to have God's Spirit upon us (1 Peter 4:14);
- to make our hearts better (Ecclesiastes 7:3);
- to make us humble (Deuteronomy 8:2);
- to make us perfect (1 Peter 5:10);
- to preserve life (Genesis 45:4-8);
- to prove that we are God's children (Hebrews 12:6,7).

Beloved, do not be amazed *and* bewildered at the fiery ordeal which is taking place to test your quality, as though something strange — unusual and alien to you and your position — were befalling you. But in so far as you are sharing Christ's sufferings, rejoice, so that when His glory (full of radiance and splendor) is revealed you may also rejoice with triumph — exultantly (1 Peter 4:12,13, AMP).

Why do we have to face struggles? There is a reason. As we seek to walk closer with Christ, we must recognize that nothing worthwhile comes cheaply.

The words *disciple* (a pupil or follower) and *discipline* (training that develops self-control, character or efficiency; submission to authority or control) come from the same Latin root, *discapere* (to hold apart). One cannot be a true disciple without becoming disciplined. When we accepted Jesus Christ as Savior, we also began a process that would make us more like Him.

TACKLING TROUBLE

So what should we do when troubles strike? Do we turn and run from the problems? The most difficult troubles with which we deal are those that are unexpected, undeserved and undiagnosed. But we aren't helpless. We have options. We can go beyond our natural circumstances and tap into supernatural strength.

When we're faced with problems, we must first get control of self. The natural reaction is to panic, lose control, complain, feel sorry at being "victimized" and withdraw. To cope, we must refuse feelings of self-pity and overcome resentment, revenge and ill-will.

Asking God for wisdom, we must then look for a reason for the trouble. If the reason isn't clear (most of the time, whether we accept it or not, it is), we need to look for the purpose. Reason and purpose are slightly different. Purpose implies a plan: "What can I learn or how can I benefit from this situation? What do I need to do to turn this trouble into a triumph?"

Acting supernaturally, we have the power to rebuke Satan from taking control of our lives: "Submit yourselves therefore to God. Resist the devil, and he will flee from you" (James 4:7). Submissiveness to God involves trusting Him for the patience to endure and the power to cope: "In all these things we are more than conquerors through him that loved us" (Romans 8:37).

We don't have to wallow around in the mire, chins dragging on the ground and brows furrowed, merely to prove that we're spiritually minded. That's not successful Christianity. But neither should we think that life in Christ is going to be the proverbial bed of roses. That line of thinking is neither mature nor realistic. As long as we seek to follow Jesus Christ, the struggle will continue.

A MYSTERY

Life is a mystery. Life itself, from beginning to end, cannot be explained totally. Only God understands what brings the initial spark of life. Only the Master Designer holds the answers to all of life's questions.

Life is a gift from God. There is nothing more precious.

Life is a race. It involves preparation, struggle and reward.

Life is a journey. As travelers, we spend our time in observation, experience and continual progress.

Life is uncertain. No one except God knows what the content or the length will be.

Life on earth is brief. It is, according to the Bible, like a vapor, a flower, a candle and soon-withered grass.

Life after the grave, however, is eternal. Death does not end all. In many ways, death is just the beginning. "For I reckon that the sufferings of this present time are not worthy to be compared with the glory which shall be revealed in us" (Romans 8:18).

Life on earth is a one-way street, and each day we pass signposts we'll never see again (tragic events, special moments, fulfilled dreams, shattered hopes). But though tomorrow is uncertain, there are three great anchors in life:

Believing God.
Belonging to God.
Serving God.

The person anchored therein possesses the power to cope with whatever struggles he may face.

Most of the passengers on the jet were uneasy as they sped along through a dark, fierce, stormy night. Lightning flashed all around. The massive plane lurched

156

again and again. Fear and tension among the passengers became thick enough to cut.

One young boy who was sitting all by himself in one of the front seats, however, seemed utterly unaware of the storm thrashing outside the windows. He didn't seem to mind the tense, life-threatening situation. Instead, he was busy with other activities.

Finally one of the passengers said to the boy, "Sonny, I see that you're all alone on the plane. Aren't you afraid to travel like this on such a stormy night?"

The lad looked up with an impish grin and answered confidently, "No, I ain't afraid. You see, my daddy's the pilot!"

POWER PRINCIPLES

I can cope with the struggles of life through a realistic evaluation of the causes, searching for solutions, not scapegoats.

I can release any problems I face by first understanding that God has a design for my life, that He will forgive me when I fail and that He will help me forgive those who have wronged me.

I must rely on God to help me cope with life's struggles, always realizing He is more interested in my growth than in my comfort.

I can strengthen my ability to cope by reaching out to others in the midst of their crucial struggles.

A POWER PROMISE

Wherefore seeing we also are compassed about with so great a cloud of witnesses, let us lay aside every weight, and the sin which doth so easily beset us, and let us run with patience the race that is set before us, looking unto Jesus the author and finisher of our faith; who for the joy that was set before him endured the cross, despising the shame, and is set down at the right hand of the throne of God. For consider him that endured such contradiction of sinners against himself, lest ye be wearied and faint in your minds (Hebrews 12:1-3).

A PRAYER FOR POWER TO COPE WITH LIFE

Heavenly Father, I give myself to you — body, soul and spirit. The Word that I study and confess will not return empty or without result.

I know that You are looking for followers who are willing to mature. I want to be one of those who is rightfully called by Your name.

I accept Your design and inner working. My life, my dreams, my hurts, my insufficiencies, my wants — I give all to You. And I will give You all the glory for whatever You do through me. Amen.

NOTES

Chapter 2
1. Arthur Hardy, "Phobias in Our Society," *USA Today* (April 23, 1985), p.C1.
2. Hardy, *USA Today*

Chapter 3
1. Helen Keller, *The Story of My Life* (New York: McMillan and Company, 1974), p.142.

Chapter 6
1. Richard S. Lazarus, "Understanding Psychological Man," *Psycology Today* (May 1982), pp. 43,44.

Chapter 10
1. G. Sidney Buchanan, *Morality, Sex, and the Constitution* (Lanham, MD: University Press of America, 1985), p. 211.
2. Mel White, *Lust: The Other Side of Love* (Old Tappan, NJ: Fleming H. Revell Co., 1978), p.15.
3. White, *Lust: The Other Side of Love*

Chapter 14
1. Billy Graham, *The Jesus Generation* (Minneapolis: Worldwide Publications, 1971), p. 102.